WORKSHOP 1
by and for teachers

WRITING AND LITERATURE

edited by
Nancie Atwell

HEINEMANN
Portsmouth, New Hampshire

HEINEMANN
A division of Reed Publishing (USA), Inc.
361 Hanover Street, Portsmouth, NH 03801-3912
Offices and agents throughout the world

We wish to thank the following for permission to reprint previously published material:

From Jane Yolen, *Owl Moon*, illustrated by John Schoenherr (New York: Philomel Books, 1987). Reprinted by permission of Philomel Books.

From Langston Hughes, "Poem," *The Dream Keeper and Other Poems*, copyright 1932 by Alfred A. Knopf, Inc., and renewed 1960 by Langston Hughes. Reprinted by permission of Alfred A. Knopf, Inc.

Every effort has been made to contact the copyright holders and the children and their parents for permission to reprint borrowed material. We regret any oversights that may have occurred and would be happy to rectify them in future printings of this work.

ISBN 0-435-08492-5
ISSN 1043-1705
Designed by Wladislaw Finne.
Printed in the United States of America
10 9 8 7 6 5 4 3

CONTENTS

ABOUT
WORKSHOP 1

*W*orkshop is the brainchild of Donald Murray. Two years ago he wrote to Philippa Stratton at Heinemann and suggested a new annual publication about the teaching of writing and reading in which "the title, the direction, and the tone should all focus on classroom teachers talking to classroom teachers." He recognized the need for a journal that would help concerned teachers who feel professionally isolated and are seeking a vigorous connection to other teachers of writing and reading, and he proposed that a teacher serve as its editor. If ever anybody needed one more bit of evidence that Donald Murray is a remarkable friend to teachers, the existence of *Workshop* should cinch it.

I was both glad and terrified when Philippa approached me about editing the annual. I saw myself as one more professionally isolated teacher and tried to imagine launching a journal from an island in Maine. The terror evaporated when I sent out a call for manuscripts for the first volume and began to receive phone calls, letters, and manuscripts from teachers throughout the United States and Canada. Their responses created an instant professional community of teacher-researchers, and I found myself a participant in the very best kind of teachers' room talk. My new colleagues are careful observers of students' learning and their own teaching. As teacher-researchers, they write with rich specificity and a solid grounding in theory. They avoid gimmicks and prescriptions. They read—academic texts but also contemporary and classic novels, criticism, poetry, history, and children's literature. Their classrooms are reading and writing

5

workshops, open-ended yet stable environments that invite the highest degree of literacy. I called the publication *Workshop* because I hope it will share the characteristics of this special context in which literate professionals view both learning and teaching as unfolding processes.

Each volume of *Workshop* will feature a dozen or so articles by teacher-researchers representing grades K–8, a discussion between an expert teacher and a professional leader, an article by a writer of children's books, and an interview with another children's author that is designed to be shared with young readers and writers. To provide teachers with specific information that they might integrate in their classrooms and explore with colleagues and students, each volume of *Workshop* addresses one theme. The theme of *Workshop 1* is Writing and Literature.

The phrase "the reading-writing connection" has become a commonplace in professional journals, conference programs, and publishers' catalogues over the past few years (suffering a fate similar to that of those other monoliths, "The Writing Process" and "Whole Language"). The link is often so watered down and meager that "the reading-writing connection" is invoked to yoke context-stripped writing exercises to context-stripped reading activities.

In contrast, the contributors to this volume examine what is possible when teachers who understand real reading and real writing bring them together so that students may engage in and enjoy both, draw naturally and purposefully on their knowledge of both, and discover what the authors and readers of a variety of genres actually do. These teachers of reading have abandoned basals in favor of literature, acknowledging the role that wonderful stories, themes, and language play in learning to read. As teachers of writing, they have dismantled what Tom Newkirk has called "the writing ghetto" by recognizing the role that literature can play in learning to write. They agree with Frank Smith (1983): "the writing that anyone does must be vastly complemented by reading if it is to achieve anything like the creative and communicative power that written language offers."

The goal of *Workshop 1: Writing and Literature* is to show what is possible when teachers "vastly complement" students' writing by adopting approaches that draw rigorously on a wealth of children's literature. In the opening article Linda Rief demonstrates how her own literacy—her rich, personal knowledge of writing and literature—enables her eighth graders to write and read everything under the sun, and how their writing and reading then becomes her language arts curriculum. Barbara Faust, who teaches pre–K and kindergarten, follows one little boy who is under the spell of Vera B. Williams and shows how his collaboration with the author/illustrator propelled his own emerging literacy, as well as her own awareness of the effects of good talk about good books in creating a climate for literacy among preschool children. Ann M. Martin, author of the popular Babysitters Club series (Scholastic), shares correspondence she has received from her young readers. The letters demonstrate the humor, voice, and sense of purpose that emerge when individual children take it upon themselves to write to authors of books they have chosen for themselves—a far cry from class letter-writing assignments. Martin also provides tips for children who want to write to favorite authors.

Looking for ways that first-grade reading and writing might take on purpose and meaning, Daniel Meier describes a writing exchange between his class and children at a school in Oxford, England. Daniel is convinced that even the youngest writers and readers seek and deserve genuine communication, and convincingly argues that primary teachers must find ways to foster social contexts that promote engagement with text.

I have long been a fan of Jack Wilde, fifth-grade teacher and a summer instructor at the University of New Hampshire, and I was delighted when he agreed to talk with Tom Newkirk for *Workshop*. In their interview, Jack describes his methods for connecting reading and writing in teaching poetry and persuasion, tells of lessons he has learned through his own interviews with Newbery Medalist Katherine Paterson, and reminds language arts teachers of the big picture.

Donna Skolnick is a writing resource teacher. Her teaching of writing, both whole group mini-lessons and individual conferences, draws extensively on her knowledge of children's books and authors. She shares a variety of ways in which she and her colleagues have used particular works of literature to "illuminate the writer's craft" during writing workshop.

In their articles Cora Five and Marna Bunce focus on the reading and writing of poetry. Cora recounts her experience of the past school year when, as a longtime, successful teacher of writing workshop, she started to read poetry to her fifth graders. She shows how she and her kids came to understand, compose, and love poetry because she took the plunge and dismantled her own "prose ghetto." Marna, an experienced reader and teacher of poetry, highlights the poetic language and techniques she finds in picture books, helping children to bridge the gap between prose and poetry. She also describes how each of her students creates a poetry thesaurus as a source of beautiful language for use in writing, and how she taps poetry in writing conferences.

Kathleen Moore looks at fiction in the writing workshop. When her second and third graders, avid readers of fiction, avoided writing it, Kathleen turned them loose with their favorite books and an assignment: "What 'works' in the books you read?" When her children then wrote their own fiction, they drew on knowledge of the genre that they had discovered and articulated for themselves.

Three of the contributors to *Workshop 1* examine writing and reading outside the language arts program. Pat Greeley, a fifth-grade teacher, wove together reading, writing, and social studies by asking her students to read and write historical fiction about the westward movement of the 1800s. Their reading and writing made history personal for her students. It also enriched the content of their historical knowledge as they gathered and discussed specific information about a particular time and place. Carol Avery describes an impromptu social studies project that began as a role-play on building the Great Wall of China but ended as an emblem of the interplay of talk, collaboration, reading, and writing that made her first-grade classroom a community of learners. Rena Moore examines relationships among reading, writing, and science in the context of a study of fossils, in a classroom in which all learning is hands-on and process based. Rena draws parallels between the discomfort many teachers feel about teaching science and the similar lack of confidence they experienced as novice teachers of writing, and proposes a science workshop that, like writing and reading workshops, allows the teacher and students to learn together.

For this premier volume of *Workshop*, Mary Ellen Giacobbe interviewed the husband and wife team of Carol and Donald Carrick. Her article focuses on their work habits—she as an author, he as a writer and illustrator—and the extensive research that lies behind their books for children. Mary Ellen comes away with a compelling message for teachers to share with young writers: write however you need to but first, know your topic. Carol Brennan follows up with an account of Authors' Day at her middle school and describes the connections students and teachers made when three authors visited the school and talked frankly about their craft. And Karen Weinhold concludes *Work-*

shop 1 with a series of snapshots of eighth graders whose lives are changed because they have spent a year with a teacher who believes and acts as if they are competent readers, writers, and human beings.

As I read and reread the articles that comprise *Workshop 1*— as well as the fine submissions for which there simply wasn't space—I was struck by the special nature of workshop teachers' experience, both in and out of the classroom. They know and love writing and literature, and they bring this knowledge and passion to their teaching. In conferences and mini-lessons they offer explicit advice that allows students to discover and act on their own intentions as readers and writers, advice students trust because they see their teachers as readers and writers.

In contrast, a recent, widely cited text (Hillocks 1986) characterizes the workshop methods associated with Donald Graves and Lucy Calkins as "reactive" approaches that "provide a low level of structure and are nondirectional about the qualities of good writing" (119). It is a mystery to me what classroom this picture of the workshop model is based on: I cannot recognize in it the *pro*active stance taken by the contributors to this volume. And I wonder if our profession lacks a frame of reference for thinking about workshop approaches, which in fact depend on highly structured *environments* rather than assignments, and on constant talk about the qualities of good writing, but *in the context of pieces of student writing and children's literature.* The expertise of the contributors to *Workshop 1* lies not in designing writing assignments—although they do, on occasion and with well-considered reasons, assign writing—but in their thoroughgoing knowledge of how writers write and readers read, of excellent children's literature, of the individual children they teach, and of ways to encourage and direct young writers. The articles in *Workshop 1* demonstrate high student initiative, but coupled with high teacher initiative in a way that cheers me immeasurably. The authors' goals for their students go beyond the successful completion of a writing assignment to the development of an insider's understanding of how good writing works—to, as Jack Wilde concludes, "experiences that are so rich . . . they'll help sustain a child for life."

I look forward to submissions to the next volumes of *Workshop*, "Beyond the Basal" and "The Politics of Process," for which a call for manuscripts appears at the end of this collection. I anticipate many new opportunities to learn from my literate colleagues everywhere, and from their literate students.

Finally, I am grateful to Donald Murray, both for conceiving *Workshop* and getting me started, to Philippa Stratton and Donna Bouvier for their good counsel and good humor, to Lynn Irish for clearing the way, and to Don Graves, who always listened.

N. A.

Southport Island, Maine

References

Hillocks, George, Jr. 1986. *Research on Written Composition.* Urbana, Ill.: National Council of Teachers of English.

Smith, Frank. 1983. "Myths of Writing." In *Essays into Literacy*, 81–88. Portsmouth, N.H.: Heinemann.

Reader and writer, we wish each other well. Don't we want and don't we understand the same thing? A story of beauty and passion, some fresh approximation of human truth?

Eudora Welty

SEEKING DIVERSITY: READING AND WRITING FROM THE MIDDLE TO THE EDGE

LINDA RIEF
Oyster River Middle School
Durham, New Hampshire

O n the first day of school in my eighth-grade classroom I explain what we can expect of each other as learners, how the room is organized, and why I do what I do. A hand shoots up and Shawn asks, "Lemme get this straight. You mean we get to *read* during reading, and *write* during writing?"

Within three days Shawn has read *Wild Cat* by Robert Newton Peck ("kinda gross when the babies get eaten"), *The Cat Who Went to Heaven* by Elizabeth Coatsworth ("I think I gotta read this one again—I was kinda confused"), and *Of Mice and Men* by John Steinbeck ("If the smart guy didn't have the dumb guy taggin' along, I think he coulda gotten a job easier . . . I think he feels bad for him though").

What do these books have in common? They are all thin. At this point, it is Shawn's only criterion for choosing books. At fifteen, he is in eighth grade for the third time and confesses to me that he has never read a book in his life.

"Yo, Mrs. Rief, I'm three [books] for three [days]. Better get more [thin] books," Shawn smiles as he fingers through the shelves of paperbacks.

At our team meeting that afternoon, the resource room teacher reads from Shawn's record at previous schools. She tells me that Shawn *hates* reading and writing, has real problems with both, and not to expect much. If he is backed into a corner, she reports, he becomes belligerent. I thank her for the information, wondering what Shawn's former teachers considered reading and writing.

September ninth, the fourth day of school. Sitting at round tables or on large pillows scattered throughout the room, we are all reading or writing. Shawn sits at a table on my left. I watch as he bends over his reading log, his thick hands writing furiously. He finishes, leans over, pokes me in the arm, and says, "Read this. This guy's pretty good."

I tuck my finger into the page I'm reading from *One Child* by Torey Hayden, and Shawn hands me a Great Brain book. The part he wants me to read explains how the Great Brain solved the mystery because he realized that glasses fog up in a warm room after being out in the cold, so the person couldn't have seen what he claimed he saw. Shawn laughs. "That happens to me all the time. This guy's pretty good." I chuckle in agreement.

Sandy sits on my right. She turns the book she is reading upside down on the table, opens her reading log, and writes:

> Sept. 9
> 30 min.
> p. 13–36
> *Toward a Psychology of Being*

What I think he is saying is that a healthy person [who] wants to grow wants to be more independent and more self-reliant. Growth-motivated people aren't directed by their environment or social conditions. I haven't really understood what Maslow has been talking about cuz he keeps mentioning existentialism and I have no idea what that is. Usually, though, by the first eighty pages everything begins to fall into place and I can read a lot faster because I know what the author is talking about and I don't have to keep reading paragraphs over and over. If I still don't understand what's being said I read on and sooner or later it falls into place.

Sandy and Shawn may be at very different ends of the ability spectrum, but they have one important thing in common. They are genuine readers and writers bringing meaning to, and taking meaning from, their chosen texts. In four days they understand clearly what I'm after: teach me what you know, how you've come to know that, and what you are able to do with that knowledge. Sandy and Shawn will challenge me throughout the year —Shawn, to keep him reading, writing, and thinking about his learning and Sandy, to keep up with her intellectually, and to nudge her to teach me more. It doesn't matter at what level these students appear to be. My job is to guide them beyond what they can already do, to challenge them to challenge themselves.

Could I address Sandy's and Shawn's needs with a teacher's

manual or with workbooks aimed at the "average" eighth grader? Of course not. Workbooks don't address the unique learning styles, the extraordinary ideas, the honest thinking, or the prior knowledge each child brings to the classroom. My students are my curriculum. I want to nurture that uniqueness, not standardize my classroom so that the students become more and more alike, their only aim to pass minimum competency tests.

Neither can I separate reading, writing, speaking, and listening. They are integrated processes finely woven into a tapestry of literacy. The components of language have to be taught as a whole for learning to be meaningful. Each aspect of language use enriches another. I immerse my students in good literature and provide continual occasions for writing and talking so they can begin to answer their biggest questions—Who am I? Why am I here?—through their reading and writing.

Sandy and Shawn are only two of the reasons we are all learners in the classroom: there are 105 others. We all have names and, like Sandy and Shawn, we all have our own, unique voices. Don Murray suggests that we should seek "diversity in writing, not proficient mediocrity." I'm seeking that same diversity in reading, too.

For learning to be meaningful for each of us, I have to see my students as individuals. I can only hear the diverse voices by offering them choices, giving them time, and responding to their reading and writing (Giacobbe 1985). Most importantly, I must model my own process as a learner. So I write with my students and read with them. At the end of every year I ask students, "If you had to pick the one thing I did that helped you the most as learners, what would it be?" They inevitably say, "You write with us and you read with us."

All teachers should be readers and writers, but teachers of language arts *must* be writers and readers. How many schools hire home economics teachers who do not cook or sew, industrial arts teachers who will not use power tools, coaches who have never played the game, art teachers who do not draw, Spanish teachers who cannot speak Spanish? Yet, how many prospective English teachers are asked in their interviews, "What are you reading? What are you writing?"

When I first began teaching, my students read and wrote in my voice, because they answered my questions. Then I asked myself what made writing and reading easy for me, and I realized that to express themselves effectively all learners have to read and write and speak in their own voices. But their voices can only come from answers to their own questions, their own inquiries. Now I constantly ask my students, "What do *you* think?" as they read and write.

Richard Rodriquez, author of *Hunger of Memory*, once told an audience at a luncheon in Texas, "Listen to my voice and wonder how it comes to be." We must do the same with our students: listen to their unique voices and ask how they have come to be. It is not easy to encourage such diversity in our classrooms. It takes time for students to find their own voices and their own texts. And it requires us to trust that students do have important things to say.

I expect good reading and writing in which one process enriches the other, in which students' ideas and wonderings invite risks and take them to the outer edges of what they know and what they can do. I expect good reading and writing, in which process and product are woven tightly into literate tapestries of wonder and awe.

My students seldom disappoint me.

While we were reading from *The Diary of Anne Frank* together, I read aloud from Elie Wiesel's *Night* and from several children's books, including *Rose Blanche* by Roberto Innocenti and *Hiroshima No Pika* by Toshi Maruki. In my reading log I wrote:

> Just finished *Night* by Wiesel. I felt tears lumping in my stomach, in my throat, tightening my whole body. I don't think I would have been so upset by this book if Mom hadn't died a year ago. I felt Wiesel's relief when his father died, a burden relieved, yet he loved his father so much. After taking care of Mom with my sisters all summer I felt a burden relieved. Yet, in the moment it was over I wanted her back. Wiesel's last two sentences haunt me: "From the depths of the mirror, a corpse gazed back at me. . . . The look in his eyes, as they stared into mine has never left me" (p. 109). I wonder if the look of his father has ever left him?

In response to *The Inner Nazi*, which she chose to read on her own, Sandy wrote in her log:

> I wonder why I am so drawn to Hitler's insanities, and not the Jews' suffering? It's not that I sympathize with the Nazis, but I think it has something to do with "evil" always being more interesting than "good." . . . After WW II, everyone said "Oh, that won't happen again, we won't let it" but it is happening . . . all over the world (S. Africa). It really makes me wonder, when Americans come together, we write letters, make phone calls, demonstrate, petition and protest

when Coke changes its formula, but we can't end apartheid in South Africa.

The poems Sandy was writing reflected a strong connection with her reading:

Television Pogrom

Numb with indifference
I watch
rows and columns of goose-stepping figures
move across the screen
in the comfort of my own home
the horrors
of the camps
flicker on the mocking glass bubble
Then
as if a dose of reality might be
too much
it's a break to suburbia
where a trim woman
tells me to use lemon-brite on my
no-wax floors.

Sandy Puffer

Sandy played with poetry to make connections between what she read and what she knew. I tried poetry because Sandy taught me how to take the risk. In one poem, both Wiesel's *Night* and my mother were still on my mind.

Waiting for Her to Die

I change
dressings cleanse wounds
measure medicines mash foods
launder sheets plump pillows
vacuum rugs scrub floors
scour tile dust knick-knacks
mend curtains repair furniture
mow grass trim hedges
plant shrubs arrange flowers
and tiptoe
tiptoe so I won't
wake her "don't
tiptoe just because my eyes are closed"
she whispers from the hospital bed in her livingroom
so I don't
but I do

wash windows so that
she and I
can see clearly.

I also wrote a letter to Elie Wiesel, because I was personally touched by his words, and shared it with the class.

Dear Mr. Wiesel,

    I just finished reading your book *Night*. It made me weep inside. It is so clear how much you loved your father. You took me back with you as you gazed at his face. I reached out to touch him as I was reading your words. For this book alone you deserve the Nobel Peace Prize, for you are not letting people forget.

    I could not help but think of my mom as I read the page on your father's death. My mom battled cancer for five years. By the time she died there was little left to her body. Her eyes were those of a corpse—one who fought too long. I took turns with my two sisters taking care of her all summer. Her last words were, "Lin, be careful driving home. I love you." I was relieved to leave. She died before I made it home. I had no time to ask her back.

    What you went through is terrifying. What you went through with your dad is heartbreaking. You must wake at night "lying in the bunk at Buchenwald." I'm so sorry you had to suffer so much.

    I read somewhere that you write so no one will forget. I will not let my students forget either. Thank you for writing this book.

Melissa wrote a letter to Farley Mowat, not because it was a class assignment but because she had legitimate questions she wanted answered.

Dear Mr. Mowat,

    I am an eighth grade student in the Oyster River Middle School.

    I have recently read your book *A Whale for the Killing* and found that I had many questions when I was finished. Was the whale really pregnant? What happened to you after the whale was gone? Did people forget about the whale or do most people still remember her? What did they do with the whale after she died?

    The biggest question that I have would be: In the time that you were trying to help the whale, did you ever doubt yourself? Did you ever think about giving up? turning away?

    I think you did a very brave thing in saving the whale. I'm proud of you and I hope you are proud of yourself.

    Thank you so much for writing that book. In it you have answered many of my questions, and I hope you will answer these. Thank you for reading my letter.

                    Sincerely,
                    Melissa Geeslin

Andy, who read science fiction and fantasy voraciously (Margaret Weis and Tracy Hickman, Douglas Adams, Piers Anthony), tried on the styles of the authors he was reading as he wrote descriptive pieces like "Night Walk."

> We donned our jackets, chose our walking sticks, and embarked on our journey into the College Woods. . . . On our way we decorated our staves . . . my staff was decorated with a lush green fern, two bright red cardinal feathers, and three blue jay feathers, along with a shiny plate of mica, and a pure white rock. I wrote ancient runes and glyphs with crushed berry juice. My most prized possession was a collection of porcupine quills that dangled from leather thongs attached to the crest of my staff . . .
>
> Andy Reiff

While many students were more comfortable writing real-world nonfiction, Andy focused on science fiction and fantasy. When I asked him how his writing was going one day in a roving conference, he told me casually that he was "writing for a magazine." He had practiced enough: on his own he had sent a query letter to the editor of *DUNGEON Adventures* proposing an "idea for a series of three modules" in which he discussed plot, characters, and possibilities. The letter was complex, well-organized, and thoughtful. Inspired by his own compelling purposes, Andy joined the real world of writers.

Gillian reached beyond the classroom too. After tucking a painful story about her father into her working folder, she turned to one about a fishing trip with her grandfather. The last paragraphs read:

> . . . I can see the tip of the fish's head over the side of the boat. It breaks through the water like a groundhog poking his nose through fresh, spring soil. Opa bends down and with one swift movement, scoops the fish into the net. My first fish—a little six-inch sunfish.
>
> I use the rest of my strength to paddle home. I need to tell Grandma about the "whale of a fish" I caught, before Opa comes up the path, carrying the truth.
>
> Gillian Nye

Scholastic Scope bought and published Gillian's story. She, too, was on her way to knowing that she is a real writer. In time, she will work again on the piece about her father.

Because my students try fiction and nonfiction, I do too. I need to know what makes different kinds of writing work so I can help students see the differences. But I hated the science fiction I wrote. It made no sense; I didn't want anyone to read it. If my students are going to try science fiction, they will have to seek responses from each other. I will have to find other ways of helping them, perhaps by reading more science fiction or by finding someone who understands the genre.

I tried realistic fiction to exaggerate the truth. My lead to "Reunion" begins:

> She didn't give much thought to him as she entered the crowded country club hall. But as she plunged into an ocean of bobbing heads and waves of laughter, it was his face she recognized. Her mind, like a videotape on rewind, darted backwards and replayed the scene twenty years earlier when she had last seen him . . .
>
> . . . She surveyed the still life as she would a Norman Rockwell painting. Pink plastic curlers rolled tightly in her hair. A crying baby wriggling in her arms. A toddler clinging precariously to a fistful of jeans. And his face, this same face, as she opened the front door. A surprise visit. He didn't tell her he was on his way to Vietnam. He didn't tell her he came to say goodbye. He didn't tell her he was scared. She didn't ask him where he had been for three years. She didn't tell him how worried she had been, how much she had missed him. She didn't need to tell him she hadn't waited this time. She only remembered his words, "Sorry I . . . I missed your husband. You take care," and he was gone.

And I tried nonfiction. My lead to "First Love" begins:

> Bryan, my seventeen-year-old son, slams open the back door and swaggers down the hallway. He wraps his arm around my shoulders and announces triumphantly, "Mom, wait'll you see the bargain I got. Why the wheels alone are worth two hundred dollars!"

Immersed in reading and writing in all genres for their own genuine purposes, my students take on serious issues. Often I don't know where their ideas come from. I suspect that some come from sharing each other's drafts and from the books they read, and that others come from the literature I share with them, the topics I'm writing about, or the occasional exercises I ask them to try. But most of their ideas are their own. Because they know they will write and read every day, writing topics and books they want to read are constantly on their minds. They read as writers and write as readers. Sarah says, "The more you read, the better you can find words to describe what you're talking about."

"I get a lot of stuff from the books I read," says Andy. "I just kind of record it in my brain—like describing words and vocabulary—and *ideas* definitely. It might be something the author says . . . just that little bit of information might inspire me or just trigger something in my mind to try to expand on."

"The more you read," says Jessie, "the more you get different styles of writing, and you can bring them together as your own . . . and things you don't like you can try to avoid in your own writing."

Jeremy ties it all together. As a writer, "if you want to please the reader, then you gotta read what the reader is reading."

Sometimes they can't let go of topics and go back again and again to issues that are important to them. A trip to a local nursing home stayed with Karen for a long time. She drafted this poem in her head for a long while, then wrote it down with few revisions:

The Nursing Home
They reach out,
    wrinkled,
        dying hands
  in desperation
To touch
    swiftly passing people.
I see
  their pain
But
  am scared
    by vacant eyes
  and walk by.
I hear stories
    of lives
  lived long ago,
But
  do not want
    to get involved.
So
  I listen,
    out-of-place,
  to tales issuing
    from gaping mouths
And leave,
  with guilt
    and relief.
          Karen Gooze

In a lighter vein, Emily used language playfully when she borrowed the style of Marc Gallant's *More Fun with Dick and Jane*:

James Loves to Read
by Emily Walenta

See James read. James loves to read.

    Read, James, read.

    "What are you reading, James?" Emily asks.

    James says, "Oh, oh, oh! You will never know!"

    "Look, Emily, look at what James is reading," says Alison. "It is a Playboy!"

    "Oh, James," says Alison. "You are a bad boy!"

    James turns to Alex. "Alex, look at that! Wow! Wow! Wow!"

    "You guys are crazy!" says Emily. "You should not have brought that to school."

    "See James read," says his teacher. "James loves to read."

In our classroom we are constantly playing with language: we *immerse* ourselves in language when we read, write, speak, and listen. We read children's literature, adolescent fiction, mysteries, nonfiction, poetry, newspapers, magazines, plays, fantasy—anything and everything that is good literature, literature that I love and literature the students love. We write letters, poetry, essays, personal narratives, short stories, sports articles, even novels—anything and everything that is important to us. We talk about what makes good writing and about how we solve our reading and writing problems. We laugh, cry, and enjoy. In our classroom we are all learners, and we are all teachers.

My curriculum is controlled by the students—not by some publisher in a distant city who thinks all students should learn the same things, not by some administrator who doesn't trust the teacher as a literate human being.

    Yet, teachers need to trust themselves as learners too. At an NCTE Spring Conference in Boston I noticed a publisher's display table surrounded by a throng of teachers. Thinking only a well-known author could draw such a crowd, I stood back, hoping to catch a glimpse of Chris Van Allsburg, Lois Lowry, or Robert Cormier. But there was no author at this display. Instead, I discovered that teachers were shoving and pushing to get the publisher's answer to all our educational woes: teachers' manuals for Cliff Notes. Publishers will continue to control our classrooms with this nonsense as long as we continue to buy it.

Another publisher's representative must have seen the look of disappointment on my face, and misread it. He pointed to a nearby table and said, "Here, we have manuals for *Velveteen Rabbit* and *Charlotte's Web* filled with comprehension questions, tests. . . ."

"Why?" I interrupted. "Whatever happened to real reading and honest writing?"

He turned to a paying customer.

Just as I settle back into my book, *The Education of Little Tree* by Forrest Carter, a teacher cranes his head around the frame of my door. He steps over sprawled bodies, bends down, and whispers to me, "Boy, you sure planned hard for this lesson."

I am somewhat annoyed by this interruption, but take the time to glance around the room. There is hardly a sound. Marissa and Missy are propped against one wall on a pillow. Marissa turns a page of *The Great Gilly Hopkins*. Missy's face is intent, almost worried, as she reads *Go Ask Alice*. Julie cradles *Taking Terri Mueller* in her lap. George is halfway through *Never Cry Wolf*.

Mandy and Jen are conferring quietly over a piece of writing about Mandy's grandmother. Val is revising a mystery piece she "just got an idea for." Brandon, who has just read *It Was a Dark and Stormy Night*, is writing out some of his own best "worst" leads for the Bulwer-Lytton "bad" writing contest.

There is a commotion in the hallway as students pass. Across from us, the class is very loud while they wait for the teacher. Pat, one of my eighth graders, stands and walks slowly to the door, stepping over classmates, eyes remaining fixed on *One Child*. He reaches out, feels for the knob, and pulls the door shut, never missing a word as he and Sheila, the main character, sink back down into his chair.

My colleague is right. I have prepared very hard for this lesson.

References

Anonymous. 1978. *Go Ask Alice.* New York: Avon Books.

Carter, Forrest. 1987. *The Education of Little Tree.* Albuquerque: University of New Mexico Press.

Coatsworth, Elizabeth. 1958. *The Cat Who Went to Heaven.* New York: Macmillan.

Frank, Anne. 1972. *The Diary of a Young Girl.* New York: Washington Square Press.

Gallant, Marc Gregory. 1986. *More Fun with Dick and Jane.* New York: Penguin Books.

Giacobbe, Mary Ellen. 1985. Reading-Writing Connection seminar. Durham, University of New Hampshire.

Hayden, Torey. 1981. *One Child.* New York: Avon Books.

Innocenti, Roberto. 1985. *Rose Blanche.* Minnesota: Creative Education.

Maruki, Toshi. 1980. *Hiroshima No Pika.* New York: Lothrop, Lee and Shephard Books.

Maslow, Abraham M. 1982. *Toward a Psychology of Being.* New York: Van Nostrand Reinhold.

Mazer, Norma Fox. 1983. *Taking Terri Mueller.* New York: Morrow.

Mowat, Farley. 1979. *A Whale for the Killing.* New York: Bantam Books.

————. 1981. *Never Cry Wolf.* New York: Bantam Books.

Murray, Donald. 1968. *A Writer Teaches Writing.* Boston: Houghton Mifflin.

Nye, Gillian. 1987. "Opa." *Scholastic Scope* 35 (24). May 18.

Paterson, Katherine. 1978. *The Great Gilly Hopkins.* New York: Avon Books.

Peck, Robert Newton. 1975. *Wild Cat.* New York: Avon Books.

Rice, Scott. 1987. *It Was a Dark and Stormy Night.* New York: Viking Penguin.

Rodriquez, Richard. 1983. *Hunger of Memory.* New York: Bantam Books.

Staudinger, Hans. 1981. *The Inner Nazi.* Baton Rouge: Louisiana State University Press.

Steinbeck, John. 1984. *Of Mice and Men.* New York: Bantam Books.

Wiesel, Elie. 1986. *Night.* New York: Bantam Books.

CASEY AND VERA B.

BARBARA Q. FAUST
Bennett Park Montessori Center
Buffalo, New York

*B*arbara, I wrote this letter to Vera B. Williams, and I want to send it to her."

"That's great, Casey. Will you read it to me?"

Vera B. Williams is the author of many wonderful children's books. Casey is the author of many wonderful stories about skateboarding. Casey enjoys Williams's books and had some things he wanted to say to her, author to author. Casey is six.

For the past three years, my three-, four-, five-, and six-year-olds have written stories and conducted research on a variety of topics, all self-chosen. What I did not see until quite recently is the power these children feel as authors. Casey—who helped compose group letters after field trips, wrote his own stories (mostly about skateboarding), read his work to the class, and published it—was an author, just like Vera B. Williams, and he knew it.

We all loved Williams's *Three Days on a River in a Red Canoe*. We read and reread it. We had favorite parts—the car driving all over the page, the shower under the waterfall, and the cat with the fish at the end. So, when I received an invitation from our librarian to attend a dinner at which Vera Williams was to speak, I accepted. I borrowed all of her books from our library, read them to the class, and told them I would be going to hear her. The children came up with a list of questions for me to ask Williams about her work and her life. They wanted to know where her story ideas came from, how she did her illustrations, whether she had any pets, how old she was.

25

Figure 1   Casey's Letter

The day of the dinner, to my great regret, I forgot the list. But that night, my greatest regret was not having the children with me. Kathy, our librarian, and I sat with Williams during dinner. She was delightful and clearly loves to write as much as my children do. Her speech, about writing and illustrating, was one the young authors I know would have loved.

When I arrived at school the next day, I was elated about what she had said and sad that the children had not heard her. I apologized to the children for forgetting their questions and told them what Williams had said about how she developed the ideas for her stories, characters, and illustrations while we reread each of the books she had talked about. I suggested that we write her a letter and enclose our list of questions.

Before we could begin, Casey came up to me with the letter he had written himself (Figure 1). His invented spelling translates:

For Vera B. Williams

Barbara
has been
reading your stories

A Chair for My Mother

to us
for weeks.

I like to write about
skateboards and you
like to write about
families. How old are you?

How do you think of your stories?

After he read me the letter I said, "Put it with the list of questions, Casey. We'll send it with the group letter."

A small group—Casey and several others—worked on the class letter to Vera Williams. They dictated while I wrote. After we finished it, we went to the office and got an envelope. When we returned to the classroom, Casey decided he wanted to write a second letter of his own (Figure 2). It reads:

Dear Vera,   Casey
(skate)   (I love Casey)
The picture that you see
is a thing that I like to
do. Could you write a
picture for me?
We sended a letter.
My ramp is in pieces.

Casey's letter-writing format changed after he worked on the group letter. This time around he included a salutation. He also chose lined paper after seeing how I had transcribed the group letter on a ruled page. He observed techniques that he could use and borrowed them for a new text of his own.

The same day, I told the children about an illustration technique Williams used on the cover of *Cherries and Cherry Pits*. She painted the main character, Bidemmi, on tracing paper, then redrew her several times. After looking at all the Bidemmis, she liked the first one best, so she cut that one out and pasted it onto a background illustration, and this became the cover. Casey came into the classroom several days later and announced, "Hey, Barb, look what I made at home!" I looked at his tiny fluorescent skaters and skateboards, drawn on paper and then carefully cut out. In my mind, I saw Vera B. Williams's Bidemmi. "What are

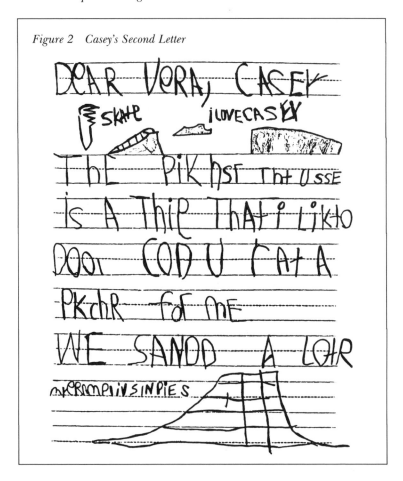

Figure 2   Casey's Second Letter

you going to do with them, Casey?" I asked. He said, "I'm gonna use 'em for a story." He wrote one of his famous skateboard stories, then pasted on the skaters and skateboards as illustrations.

Casey was only one of the young authors in my room; there were others. I thought of three-year-old Andrew's growth in confidence as he wrote and shared his stories with the class. His own pleasure was evident as he read his daily scribble stories and answered the children's questions about them. I remembered four-year-old Jeffrey's genuine relief after writing about his foster mother's stay in the hospital, a scary time for both of them. Jeffrey showed me that even young authors feel relief after writing about a difficult personal experience. I saw Caitlin's tenacity when she wrote words for her illustrations for the first time. Previously, her stories had consisted of detailed illustrations, with the words dictated to an adult. Her first solo story took a day and a half. Such tenacity! And then there was Casey and his letters to Vera B. Williams—talking, author to author, about the choice of a topic, noticing and adopting a conventional letter format and lined paper for his second letter, and appropriating her illustration technique for his skateboard story.

The children and I had become members of a literate community. We were writers—and readers, too. As readers we shared books. We reread. We discussed. ("Did you ever feel like the girl in Jeanette Caines's *Daddy?*" "Do you think Eat-It-All-Elaine ever got sick?") We told stories. Robert Munsch's *Mortimer* became "Valerie, Be Quiet!" a group participation story. Storybook characters visited our room. Harry Allard's Viola Swamp came and read *Miss Nelson Has a Field Day*—all ways of bringing children and books closer. When I accepted children as readers and writers, regardless of their level, they had no limits.

Casey was a member of this community. He responded to other writers, and others responded to him as a writer. By the time we read Williams's books, she was a writer who had a favorite subject, but so was Andrew. She was a writer who did her own illustrations, but so was Caitlin. She was a published author, but so was Casey. The closeness Casey felt to Vera B. Williams was a result of his participation in this literate community. Stories, research, and poetry were within his reach, to read and to write. Casey showed me that a writer is a writer is a writer. He knew that, and after watching him, so did I.

References

Allard, Harry. 1985. *Miss Nelson Has a Field Day*. Boston: Houghton Mifflin.

Caines, Jeanette. 1977. *Daddy*. New York: Harper & Row.

Munsch, Robert. 1985. *Mortimer*. Toronto: Annick Press.

Starbird, Kaye. 1981. "Eat-It-All-Elaine." In *Poem Stew*, ed. William Cole. New York: J. B. Lippincott.

Williams, Vera B. 1981. *Three Days on a River in a Red Canoe*. New York: Greenwillow Books.

———. 1982. *A Chair for My Mother*. New York: Greenwillow Books.

———. 1986. *Cherries and Cherry Pits*. New York: Greenwillow Books.

AN AUTHOR'S PERSPECTIVE
LETTERS FROM READERS

ANN M. MARTIN

I have never enjoyed writing letters and I'm not sure why. As an author of books for juveniles and young adults, I write approximately seventeen hundred pages each year, practically without thinking about it, but the little pile of unanswered letters on my desk daunts me. I find this ironic for more than the obvious reason: I receive about five thousand letters a year from children who have read my books. An awful lot of young letter writers are out there, and I must respond.

When I was little, children didn't write to authors very often, at least my sister Jane and I didn't, although we liked to read. Jane liked to write letters, and occasionally I would come through with one too, but we never wrote to authors. When I was eight I wrote to the producers of "Lassie" after I heard that the show was going to go off the air, to ask them please to keep it on. Someone from the network wrote back saying that it was time for the boy who played Timmy to go to college, which was terribly disillusioning, since I thought Timmy was about twelve years old. And my sister wrote to John Lindsay, the mayor of New York, to tell him she'd lost a tooth, which was surprising to my parents since we lived in New Jersey.

I think there are two reasons it never occurred to me to write to an author. For one thing, it wasn't suggested as a school assignment, as often happens today. And as far as I can remember, although I went through one of the top public school systems in the country, no children's or young-adult author came to speak at any of the schools I attended.

For another thing, I assumed that all authors were dead.

Apparently, some teachers share this feeling. Here is an excerpt from a letter I received recently from a junior high teacher.

> I wanted students to realize something that I never knew when I was growing up—authors are real people who are living today! I thought in order to be an author you had to be dead for at least 100 years because all the books I was required to read were by authors who had lived long ago.

Today kids write to authors all the time. This letter, about the books in the Baby-sitters Club series, is typical:

> Dear Ann M. Martin,
>
> I think *Kristy's Idea* [sic] is *very good*. I hope that the other books are good too. I already ordered the others but I can't find *Mary Anne Saves the Day*. I am still looking for it. I think your books are good. I am trying to read them all. I love your books. I've only read one; that is *Kristy's Idea* [sic].
>
> 1. Is it hard to be an author? 2. Where do you get your ideas for the Baby-sitters Club? 3. Is is fun being an author? 4. Do you ever get to take breaks? 5. What made you think of being an author? 6. How many years of college does it take? 7. How much do you get paid? I'll bet it's a lot. 8. How long is your work day? 9. Where do you write? 10. Are you married? 11. Do you have any pets?
>
> I know you are reading a letter from somebody you don't know so let me introduce myself. My name is Charlotte. I am 10 years old. I am in the fifth grade. I really enjoy your book about Kristy's idea. I am planning to be a baby-sitter when I grow up.
>
> Well, it is time for me to go, so bye. I would appreciate if you could write back to me. But you don't have to if it's in your way.
>
> From,
> Charlotte

However, this is not the only kind of correspondence I receive from kids. While Charlotte's letter is typical of those that children write on their own because they feel like corresponding with a favorite author, I can tell that about half of the letters I receive are written as class assignments. For the most part, these letters are short, follow some prescribed form, and lack spontaneity or imagination. Many actually end with, "P.S. If you write back I'll get an A."

Such pressure—especially for a correspondent who's going to be slow about answering. This is a typical class-assignment letter:

> Dear Miss Martin,
>
> Hi, my name is Sarah. I'm ten years old and in the fifth grade at Littlebrook Elementary School. I have brown hair and brown eyes.

In school, I read two of your books. To get our English grade we could either write a book report or write to the author. I chose to write to you. Please answer the following questions: Where did you get the ideas for *Bummer Summer* and *Inside Out*? How long did it take you to write them? How many books have you written? What was the first book you ever wrote? How did you get started writing books?

If you answer all my questions, I'll get a better grade.

Love,
Sarah

For the remainder of this article I will be concerned with those delightful letters from children who have written because they *wanted* to—because they were moved by something they read or because they were excited by what they were reading. But before I share those letters, let me explain how I've solved the dilemma of answering all my mail. When I first started receiving letters from children, they trickled in one at a time—first several each month, then several each week. I answered the letters individually and in my own handwriting, which seems to be important to children. I acquired a few pen pals that way. Now I receive too many letters to be able to answer each one with a tailor-made, handwritten reply, so I have composed a form letter that tells kids a little about myself and answers their most frequently asked questions. (However, I use stickers and a cat stamp, and sign my name with a gold pen.) This seems to do the trick—and allows every letter to receive a personal-looking response without my actually having to write five thousand letters a year. Unfortunately, I have recently had to add a P.S. to discourage pen pals, because I just can't reply to their replies, even if they are as wonderful as the following:

Dear Ann Martin,

Thank you for writing back to me! When I got your letter, I was shooting a dart gun at my cousin. It was a Friday night and my mom told me I got a letter in the mail (very rare). She said it was from New York City. Who could possibly be writing me from there?

You, of course. But I didn't know until I opened it. And when I did, I screamed and jumped up and down.

I nearly had a heart attack after finding out that there will be at least twenty-six books in the series and you're working on #19! ZONK! It took me a week to recover!

Since I'm not married and don't have any children, I have to rely on the experiences of other people's children, or on memories of my own childhood, in order to write realistically for kids. And since some of my memories are naturally outdated, and most of the children of my friends and cousins are, at the moment, seven and under, I find the letters from my readers quite enlightening. They are especially helpful in terms of what kids today are concerned with, how they express themselves, and just exactly how sophisticated they are, which isn't as sophisticated as you might think.

I'm happy to say that I've received an awful lot of letters that are purely complimentary, and it's nice to find that kids feel just as free to write to someone with a compliment as they do with a complaint, even though there is usually no incentive for doing so. Often these kids don't ask any questions, don't request a photograph of the author, and don't even expect a reply. This is my favorite such letter:

> Dear Mrs. Martin,
>
> My name is Nicole and I am a very avid reader, and really enjoy the Baby-sitters Club series. I am now in the process of reading the book #4 [sic]. Your talent for writing is so very marvelous that you should do more than four books. During the Christmas holiday I began reading your books, and those books are what made me begin to start to read again. Over the holiday I searched far and near for your book #3 and successfully found it. I have been looking for #4 for at least 2 months and I finally found it. Your books are so super I really hope you do consider writing more books for the sake of all the children who look forward for the sequel to #4. Your book has been a great success at my school in that more than half of the girls in my class have read your terrific books. I really do urge you to take this note under consideration. I am giving it to you for the sake of girls my age (11), who really do enjoy your books tremendously. Thank you!

I'm always curious to find out what in my books "speaks" to kids—what they're enjoying, or what they're relating or responding to. This comes through quite clearly in letters such as these:

> All of your main characters in The Baby-sitters Club are like me in a way. I hide my feelings like Stacey. I'm shy like Mary Anne. I'm kind of bossy like Claudia, although I don't like art shows. I'm ready and waiting like Kristy.

> I love your books. My favorite is *With You and Without You.* I know how it feels to have someone close to you die because my mom died of cancer. I had the same problem Liza did (explaining to my sister Mommy just isn't coming back). It's hard to get along without her,

but Daddy takes good care of us. Your book made me laugh at one part and cry at the next. I keep reading it over and over again. I hope you do another book about the O'Hara family.

You must think I'm crazy but is there a real Stacey McGill? I have read your Baby-sitters Club books but I fell in love with: The Truth About Stacey.

I have been having weird dreams lately about Stacey McGill. I was dreaming I went to New York to see her and she was my best friend. I don't really have a best friend but I have friends.

If there is a real Stacey could you tell me? Thanks.

From,
Erin

P.S. I would love there to be Stacey McGill.

When my mom and dad were getting a divorce I was sad and upset so I thought if I read it'll get it out of my mind. So I went to a bookstore and I saw your books. I bought the first one and read it it made me feel better and more happier. I thought I ought to tell you so you'll know that your books make people happy.

I'm intrigued by the number of children who write to me because they enjoy writing or want to become authors one day. Many of them ask for writing tips, and a number have asked for tips on how to get published.

I'm going to be a veterinarian and a writer when I get older. I practice writing here in Whitestone. I write for a monthly newspaper. I learned one important thing in writing. That is to write fiction about truth. You may do that. If *you* do, who are you in the Baby-sitters Club books? I started writing when I was six and I learned that when I was nine. I'm ten and a half now. How old were you when you started writing? I really hope you get to see this letter, not the publisher.

I wrote a book called Ups & Downs and I really want to publish it. Could you tell me where to find a publisher and editor. I'd love to publish a book. It's like my dream.

I have written my own book it is called "Super Puppies from Yuma." I named it that because it is dedicated to my grandparents and they go to Yuma Arizona every year for seven months and they have dogs that are really special to them. I published if myself.

I want to be a famous author someday and write books like you. Me and my friend are writing a newspaper and a series called *Donald The Weirdo!* Me and another friend are working on another book called *Is That a Way to Make a Friend In Maine, The Worst Place to Live?*

Many kids, even those who don't dream of becoming authors, get very caught up in whatever they're reading and write to me with ideas for sequels to books, or in the case of the Baby-sitters Club, with ideas for directions the series could take:

> Here are some suggestions for future books. You may not think they are good, but I am hoping you will like several of my ideas.
> 1. How about one of the girls getting braces? I am getting them and I hate them. Maybe I wouldn't, if one of my favorite characters had to have them.
> 2. How about a book about school problems and disappointments such as not getting cheerleader, having a misunderstanding with a teacher, or being accused of something the person didn't do but had a hard time proving she didn't?

> I hope you write one about a vampire coming out on the night of Friday the 13 and have Dawn baby-sit. Then have monsters and goons galore come out. Make Dawn call the other members to come over and help. Then solve it, that would be a good and funny book.

> Something that you might want to do in your next book is the girls decide to move farther so they can get more people [clients]. They all go to a far away job together and get kidnapped. It's just a thought.

The following excerpts simply made me laugh. All I have to say about them is that Art Linkletter was right.

> You're my favorite writer. Dr. Seuss is down the drain!

> My friends think you're fake but if you write back I will show them.

> P.S. I am thinking about writing a sequel to "GONE WITH THE WIND."

> P.S. You're famous.

> P.S. Are your characters real? If so, do you have a phone number so I can call them?

> I really like your books. You write just like a seventh grader.

> I like your book (The Baby-sitters Club) a lot. My friends and I have a club and we baby-sit Cabbage Patch dolls. . . .
> We wanted to baby-sit real children but our parents won't let us.

> Most of the girls in my 4th grade class are reading your books. Most of the boys want to too, but us girls won't let them. We're afraid they might destroy the books. They refuse to buy their own!

> Hi! I got sent to my room so I thought of you. Do you want to be pen-pals?

Hello, my name is Amy. I've read your book *The Truth About Stacey*. It's a very good book. How do you get your ideas? Are you satisfied with your career or could things be better? When is your birthday? Is this a boring letter? If so I know why, I don't really talk this way.

So how's life? What's your next book about? What are your hobbies? What was your first book? Nice talking to you.

I invite teachers of reading and writing to share this article with their kids. In closing, I'll mention several things young letter-writers can do to make the author's job of responding a bit easier:

1. Enclose a stamped, self-addressed, return envelope. Answering five thousand letters each year is expensive. The postage alone costs $1,250.
2. Include your return address and full name on the letter as well as on the envelope. Envelopes often get thrown away.
3. Date the letter. Letters take varying lengths of time to reach an author, and it's helpful to know when they were written.
4. If a reply is needed by a certain date, be sure to mail the letter at least eight weeks before that date. Letters sent to publishing companies sometimes don't reach an author right away. When they do reach the author, the author may or may not be able to respond immediately.

That's about it. Despite my reluctance to write letters, I have to say that I treasure the letters I receive from children. There's nothing as refreshing as a few original lines from an exuberant ten-year-old. The thousands and thousands of letters I've gotten are stashed in a (packed) filing cabinet in my office. They're all special, they've all been answered, and I've learned something from every one of them.

P.S. MY REAL NAME IS KIRSTIN

DANIEL MEIER
Edward Devotion School
Brookline, Massachusetts

*M*r. Leslie Stephen whose immense literary powers are well known is now the President of the London Library which as Lord Tennyson was before him and Carlyle was before Tennyson is justly esteemed a great honour. Mrs. Ritchie the daughter of Thackeray who came to luncheon the next day expressed her delight by jumping from her chair and clapping her hands in a childish manner but none the less sincerely. The greater part of Mrs. Stephen's joy lies in the fact that Mr. Gladstone is only vice-president.

Virginia Woolf wrote this report when she was ten years old. It appeared on November 21, 1892, in volume 2, issue number 45 of *The Hyde Park Gate News*, a weekly newspaper written by Woolf and her brother and sister. This neighborhood paper consisted of news articles and pieces of fiction. In the excerpt above, Woolf reports on her father, Leslie Stephen, a famous man of letters. The writing is not that of an ordinary ten-year-old, and neither is the mention of such literary greats as Tennyson and Carlyle. Her early exposure to well-known figures must have had an impact on the young Woolf, enriching her already precocious talent for reading and writing. Although Woolf's upbringing and family life were unusual, what she *did* with *The Hyde Park Gate News* can be replicated. The newspaper had a real purpose in the outside world: providing news and information, just like any adult paper.

As a teacher of first graders, I search for ways to engage my six-year-olds in writing and reading that give them, and me, a sense of purpose and meaning. Their literary texts must do something—effect some kind of change in their view of life. I must foster what Nancy Martin (1983) calls "genuine communication" in which "there is an inseparable blend of giving an account of the topic and expressing feelings about it" (155). I have the challenging, yet delightful responsibility of introducing my students to the world of writing and reading in all its possibilities—fairy tales, interviews, letters, accounts, poems, jokes, riddles, fables, stories, journals. I am the one who sets the tone, inviting the children to journey with Pooh and Piglet in search of the Woozles, or hop aboard Max's boat and sail to the fantastical land of the Wild Things. Along the way, we talk about our own trips and flights of fancy, throw them into one big pot, and then take them out to write about.

Over the course of one year my students in Brookline, Massachusetts, engaged in a letter and book exchange with a first-grade class in Oxford, England. I had met the teacher of the class on a trip to England, visited the class, and talked with the children about their reading and writing. I thought, "What a wonderful thing it would be to have the two classes write to each other and send books back and forth. Not only would the children enjoy it, but so would I."

The project consisted of an exchange of four types of material: letters dictated by the whole class to the teacher, individual letters written by the children, informational books on a topic studied by one of the classes, and books that contained stories and poetry written by the children in conjunction with a literature unit. In September I cleared off a section of a wall in my classroom and reserved it for showing the correspondence from our partner class in England.

In our group letters, the whole class brainstormed about what they wanted to write to the partner class. This process gave the beginning readers and writers in the class the same opportunity as the more advanced children to draft a letter in public and show what they could do orally. The group discussion around a text helped establish the feeling of a writing and reading community in the classroom. Whole group writing was designed to communicate with a distant audience, yet it accomplished much more. As James Britton (1982) argues, "We don't often write anything that is merely communication. There's nearly always an element of 'finding out,' of discovering" (110).

The group letters covered a range of topics: literature, writing, holidays, weather, science, special events. Here is one letter written by the class in England:

Thank you for your letter. We live in Oxford. We are in Class 7. For our Book Week we have been thinking about poems and skipping rhymes. You can see them in our mural. There's: "Policeman, Policeman Don't Catch Me," "Hopscotch," "Cat's Got the Measles," and lots more. We helped to paint the mural on our playground wall. We have sent you some photos with our names by them. We are having a good time here. Are you having a good time? Have you any snow yet?

This letter, and a photo of the mural with the painted poems, gave me the opportunity to talk with my class about the different ways that other children understand and interpret literature. It demonstrated that reading was a part of everyday life and changed my students' own perceptions of what reading and writing can do for them. This type of real communication about books allowed two different classroom communities to exchange information about the kind of literature they value. It was an exchange of literary contexts, and an enjoyable one. According to Peter Medway (1988), "maybe it will be through the pleasure of the text and not the lessons of the text that our students may best be brought into motivated engagement with reading and writing" (176).

In one letter my class sent to England, we included an anthology of our poems. Here is Katharine's:

The sun is shining on the sea,
A bird is smiling at me,
Cheep, cheep, cheep,
Sing, sing, sing,
I'll be home in just a fling,
Cheep, cheep, cheep,
Sing, sing, sing,
Me,
I'm tricking my parents,
You see!!

In another letter the partner class wrote:

We liked the book of poems that you sent us. We liked the Yellow Butter poem [a reworking of a poem by Mary Ann Hoberman] the best because it made a tongue twister. We liked it because it said black bread and it made us laugh.

My class was very proud. "Yellow Butter" was their favorite poem, too, and hearing that from the partner class strengthened their own feelings. When the partner class wrote back that they liked the poems, in effect they said to my class, "The literature you are writing is important to us, too."

The second component of the project involved the writing of individual student letters. Here, what was written was decided entirely by each student. To give a flavor of their writing voices, here are a few of the letters written to and by my class:

Dear Katharine,

How are you? My name is Kirsty. Playtime is good at school. I had a rabbit but it died. I have one brother. My brother's name is Jamie.

From
Kirsty

P.S. My real name is Kirstin.

Dear Kirsty,

I am fine. I am sorry that your rabbit died. I am half American and I am a quarter English and a quarter Australian.

Love,
Katharine

Dear Carter,

Thank you for the poems. I have two sisters and a dog. And I have lots of friends. My best friend is Nicola.

Lots of love,
Lorraine

Dear Lorraine,

Thank you for your letter. It was very nice of you to send me one. Are you having fun? I have one sister, two brothers, and one dog. My mom is an awesome cook. I like to play soccer. We are studying maps. What are you studying?

From
Carter

Dear Ann,

Hello. My name is Amy. I have a brother. His name is Adam. I like ice cream. I wish you could come to Oxford. My best friend is Sabrina.

From
Amy

Dear Amy,

My name is Ann. I know a kid named Jane that I write to in England. I am seven. I had a dog but he died.

Love,
Ann

This exchange allowed many of the children to experience letter writing, describing themselves to a distant audience they had never met, for the first time. They were forced to explain themselves to someone else, to make themselves up anew in their own words, images, and descriptions. As my students read the letters they received from the partner class, they broadened their own reading and entered into a new literary genre. This double edge made the whole project not just a simple letter exchange, but an exchange of language. According to James Britton (1982):

> As a child extends his reading, so he internalizes more and more the patterns of the written language. I don't mean that globally— and I mean many forms of the written language appropriate to many different kinds of tasks. I think this process, once we understand it, needs to be gradual. I think we can easily short-circuit it if we're too deliberate about it. I don't believe in setting the written model for their writing. I believe in reading for reading's sake and the kind of internalization that comes from reading for reading's sake will then articulate, interlink with spoken resources. (98)

Whenever I brought a package of letters from England into the classroom, my students shouted, "What did they say to us? What did they say?" The emphasis was on language, on the power of the written word to speak and convey meaning all the way across the Atlantic.

The third part of the exchange consisted of informational books and anthologies of student writing. My students wrote and sent books on such topics as spring in Massachusetts, Mexican art, whales, and dinosaurs. I asked my class to write to England and tell them about what we were studying as a way for them to organize their own thinking. Because the English class did the same thing, my students had the opportunity to see how members of another learning community represented their learning in written form. For example, here is the beginning of a book they wrote for us called "A Child's Guide to Warwick Castle":

> The first thing you see is the bridge. It goes over the dry moat. In castle days it was a drawbridge. Then you see the gatehouse and on the gatehouse wall you see the torch holder. Now you will go under the portcullis. Be careful it doesn't come down on you! Look up and you will see the murder holes. The guards threw oil and stones down on the enemy. When you go through the gatehouse you come to the second portcullis. Be careful you don't get trapped!

Most of my students had never been to England or seen a castle. This book introduced them to castles—their history, architecture, purpose, and vocabulary. This informational guide was written by children for children, a rare literary event that matches young writer to young reader.

Sending their own literature, which often corresponded with a literature unit we were working on, gave the children's writing a new dimension. The texts came alive through an extension of place and audience. Their work became published—something to be read by an audience both within and outside the world of the classroom. The children's writing took on a new kind of validity: it was their own. It also got at the true purpose of literature and art—to inform, delight, persuade, cajole, enlighten. The letter exchange, with its emphasis on saying something of value and meaning to two audiences simultaneously, is a good starting point in doing away with viewing literacy as a basic skill. The only thing that is basic here is thinking.

Reading and writing based upon what children want to say, what they want to read, what they want to write, what they want to communicate, what they want, cannot avoid being real. It has a sense of purpose that comes from within. And although I only served as facilitator between my students and the partner classroom, the project became mine too. I enjoyed it as much as the children did. The writing was theirs, but the exchange was part of the social fabric of the classroom, connecting student to student and teacher to student. When we received the book on Warwick Castle, they could see that I was learning about castle life right along with them. We were all learners. The exchange made me a "more complete teacher," to borrow a phrase from Glenda Bissex (1987, 5).

Back to Virginia Woolf, age ten:

> We think that the London Library has made a very good choice in putting Mr. Stephen before Mr. Gladstone as although Mr. Gladstone may be a first-rate politician he cannot beat Mr. Stephen in writing. But as Mr. Stephen with that delicacy and modesty which with many other good qualities is always eminent in the great man's manner went out of the room when the final debate was taking place we cannot oblige our readers with more of the interesting details.

So ends Woolf's report. Not many children could so eloquently admire and defend their own father in writing, but students in our schools can begin to write and read with the feeling that texts matter in the real world. What they need is a social context that promotes an active wrestling with literary texts—both written and oral, both distant and personal, both student generated and not. Children, especially young ones, must continually do battle with The Word. They must get to know it in all its forms and variations—kneading and rolling and slapping it into shapes that they find meaningful and, above all, enjoy.

References

Bissex, Glenda L. 1987. "What Is a Teacher-Researcher?" In *Seeing for Ourselves: Case-Study Research by Teachers of Writing*, ed. Glenda L. Bissex and Richard H. Bullock. Portsmouth, N.H.: Heinemann.

Britton, James. 1982. *Prospect and Retrospect: Selected Essays of James Britton*, ed. Gordon M. Pradl. Portsmouth, N.H.: Boynton/Cook.

Martin, Nancy. 1983. *Mostly About Writing: Selected Essays*. Portsmouth, N.H.: Boynton/Cook.

Medway, Peter. 1988. "Reality, Play, and Pleasure in English." In *The Word for Teaching Is Learning*, ed. Martin Lightfoot and Nancy Martin. Portsmouth, N.H.: Boynton/Cook.

Spater, George, and Ian Parsons. 1977. *A Marriage of True Minds: An Intimate Portrait of Leonard and Virginia Woolf*. New York: Harcourt Brace Jovanovich.

The Teacher Interview

JACK WILDE

AN INTERVIEW BY THOMAS NEWKIRK

*J*ack Wilde began his career teaching first grade in a Harlem elementary school. In 1973 he moved to Norwich, Vermont, and began teaching at the Bernice Ray School across the river in Hanover, New Hampshire, where he currently teaches fifth grade. He has been on the staff of the New Hampshire Writing Program for the past eight years. His published articles include accounts of his students' development as fiction writers (1985) and their use of a variety of genres as alternatives to the written report (1988). He recently developed a teaching unit on the writing process, *The Author's Eye* (Random House), which includes videotaped portions of an interview he conducted with novelist Katherine Paterson. Jack is currently working on a book dealing with writing instruction at the upper-elementary level.

I spoke with Jack on a Saturday morning in a house overlooking the Cape Neddick River just north of York, Maine. The river is filled and emptied by the tides, and that morning the tide was out, revealing the mud bottom littered with mussel shells. Gulls, one to a pillar, perched on the supports of an abandoned pier. We sat at the kitchen table.

TOM: Were you a reader as a child?
JACK: No.
TOM: Why not?
JACK: I'm not sure. I suspect in part because my parents weren't much at reading. As a small child my father was a farmer and my mother was trying to raise three kids and work at a job, so there wasn't much reading in the home. Also, I was and

44

remain a very slow reader. I was always conscious as a child of choosing thin books. But I can remember one year in third grade we had a teacher with a star system. You got a star for each book that you read, and a friend of mine and I set up our own competition.

I don't think I became interested in reading until the last couple years of high school, and I don't think I really became a reader until I was an adult. It was still difficult for me. I'm still a slow reader.

TOM: It's been said that the way we teach is related to our own experiences as learners. In what way is your experience as a student related to ways in which you teach?

JACK: Well, I'm sure it is related. I do not give my kids stars for the number of books that they read (although that was an impetus in my case, I think it was the wrong impetus for reading). I don't generally require them to read a certain number of books. I would much rather have the desire to read grow out of a sense of the classroom. So that's one way I can see my own experience reflected, but there are other ways in which it is not. I enjoy kids' books at this point, and most of the powerful kids' books are fiction. So if anything, I tend to steer my kids toward fiction, even though I wasn't pushed in that direction myself.

One of the things that I do is read out loud to my kids every day. I can't remember being read to after second grade. I always felt that one should read to young children, but I didn't feel that it needed to be continued. I become more convinced each year that reading aloud is very important and something we should do, certainly up through junior high and high school probably and into college.

TOM: Why do you think it's important?

JACK: There are a number of reasons. Reading aloud is a way of bridging the distance between where the child is and where you want the child to be as a reader. By using your voice as a mediator between the text and the child, you're able to make more difficult texts available to kids. And a natural reaction of a lot of children after you've read them a story is for them to read it again themselves. You've mediated it, helped make the text accessible. And I'm sure as they read it they're still hearing your voice, so your voice continues to help them.

The other reason I think reading aloud is important is that it's part of making the classroom a literate environment. Just like at home. If you read something that's really good, you want to share it—out loud. I don't just hand it to my wife and say, "Here, read this."

TOM: And in a sense it's an old notion, because the McGuffey Readers were essentially oral readers. You were supposed to read passages aloud, practice reading them aloud. So it sounds like you're getting back to that idea.

JACK: Absolutely. We've lost the old sense of "storying." You know, of sitting around in the evening and telling stories. We can recreate it to some extent in our classrooms. But I think another way of creating that same kind of ethos is by reading stories to kids. It's also an important teaching tool for me because we confer about the books that I read to them in the same way we confer about each other's writing. So it's another way to let them feel that they are on the same plane as professional authors.

TOM: How would you confer about a professional author's work? Can you give me an example?

JACK: The first thing we do is talk about what works in the text. For most of them, if they have been read to before, it's been what I call passive reading instead of active reading. There's been no engagement called for by the teacher. So, I want to establish from the first day that I expect their engagement.

Usually the first book I read aloud is *Hey What's Wrong with This One?* which is a wonderful novel about three boys whose mother has died and they're trying to find a new one. I'll read as much as I can read in fifteen minutes and then ask, "What worked for you today? What was effective?" The answers are fairly global in the beginning because they don't really have the vocabulary for it, but that's what we're about. And once we've done that with a trade book, I'll start to move in the same direction with their own writing. Later on we're going to ask questions of the author—pretend the author's there.

TOM: Do you think it's important in a reading program that the students have a common book that they all read?

JACK: Yes. My feeling is that you have to have a balance, that I want situations where six or seven kids are reading the same book. Not a basal, but a trade book. But they're also reading on their own. Last year there was one occasion where we all read one book, everybody. I think that's important because the discussion can be rich. The discussions are different if everybody is in a different book.

With groups of six or seven kids, I want them to read in certain genres. We're fortunate enough to have something like 125 titles in our library where we have at least eight copies of each book. So, I have quite a range to choose from. I'll bring in four or five sets in a genre that I want them to read. The kids are in a group, it's heterogeneous to a certain extent, and the group decides which of the five books they're going to read. So they do have some choice, it gives them practice at choosing, and we can talk about how to make good choices.

TOM: Do you have students memorize selections?

JACK: Yes.

TOM: That's again going back to an earlier notion that's out of fashion, I would say. Why do you have your kids memorize?

JACK: My kids start memorizing poetry from the first day of school, and again I have multiple reasons. One is that we're going to talk about poetry, and the kids are going to write poetry, in April or the beginning of May. I want them at that point to have a backlog, to be carrying around with them a set of poems so that they can derive a definition from this internal catalog. I'm not going to lay a definition on them or simply read a poem to them in May and say, "What's poetry? Write a poem."

I remember a poet saying that we need to treat poetry like architecture; we've got to let kids get inside of it and walk around for a while. I think that's one of my aspirations in having kids memorize poetry. Obviously one of the other things they get from it is a sense of good, strong language— of individual sentences and images.

I also want to extend their range of appreciation beyond poets like Shel Silverstein, not that he's bad. I want them to see that there are a number of different poets dealing with a number of different issues. I like it when kids tell me that they'll be walking on an October morning and think of Frost's poem:

> Oh hushed October morning mild,
> Thy leaves have ripened to the fall;
> Tomorrow's wind, if it be wild,
> Should waste them all.

They can start to see poetry not as a school subject, but as something which deals with the very heart and soul of our existence.

Because my students memorize and perform poems, it's more likely that situations will trigger words and lines. Then they'll start to have a sense of the original power that inspired, that drove Frost or Cummings to write those words.

TOM: To what extent do you think students should be asked to work within poetic structures, such as the haiku? Kenneth Koch has a number of structures that he asks students to use to begin to write poetry. Do you see value in those?

JACK: There may be some value, but I don't see it. Most of the kids fixate on the structure, so the structure takes control of the thought or experience that they're trying to convey. I realize that some poets claim that if you don't rhyme you're not allowing yourself to find the right word, that part of what a structure does is, yes, put you through certain kinds of contortions, but during the process of going through those contortions you feel for yourself that you've found the right word. So these poets experience the limitations of a prescribed structure as a positive rather than a negative.

But for kids starting out, these forms seem to limit exploration and I get a lot of singsong, a lot of superficial stuff. So my approach has been to steer away from them.

TOM: How do you begin? You have your students memorize and actively listen to poems. When you ask them to write, then, how do you initiate it?

JACK: The first thing that they do, again as a class, is to try to come up with a working definition of poetry. I don't give them a definition, they give me one. Very often my question is: What's the difference between prose and poetry? And, of course, we know as adults that there are prose poems and poetic prose, so the line isn't sharply delineated. But I ask the question to get the kids to start to discuss the qualities that they see.

Then what I've done, and this is only very recently, is to take one piece of the subjects that poetry can deal with. In other words, instead of leaving it wide open, I try to carve a niche and let them try within that niche to see what they can do. So I read them a couple of poems from *Reflections on a Gift of Watermelon Pickle*. One is called "Base Stealer" by Robert Francis, and another, "Foul Shot" by Edwin Hoey, is about the last two seconds of a basketball game. A third poem is Theodore Roethke's "Childhood on Top of a Greenhouse." All of these deal with a very short period of time, one image or one feeling, in fifteen seconds or less. I ask my kids to do the same thing. Again, acknowledging that this isn't the only subject for poetry, it's a subject that I think they can deal with, they have dealt with very successfully, because they can go back to themselves as resources. They can see that dealing with a short time frame is different from their fiction and their personal experience stories because it wouldn't blow up into a story. And they start trying to get back to their feelings, all the different ways in which they experienced those seconds, and then try to shape it into a poem.

TOM: So you work from an intensely perceived moment or set of moments. And then work from there outward into a poetic form, rather than having the poetic form be essential at the beginning?

JACK: That's right. I try to give them the sense of the lyric center. That, to me, is one of the things that makes poetry different from prose, that intense center which takes you away from the linearity that we get in most prose. What you're trying to do is to convey something that was before language, an experience that lies outside of language. Now we're going to try to bring language to it, to help recreate it for somebody else.

TOM: I know that you also connect reading and writing when you teach persuasion. How does that work?

JACK: For persuasive writing, the reading part is difficult. There's not a lot available for kids to read. Most of the editorials in local papers deal with issues that are of little interest to kids, who don't relate to zoning board disputes or questions over whether we need a new parking lot. But there are some examples, and especially letters to the editor in local papers, that my students can relate to. We read these letters and persuasive pieces my students wrote in previous years, and talk about what works and what doesn't work. Then we move into writing a persuasive piece on some issue related to our school. I limit it in this way because I've found that they write more effectively when they draw on their own knowledge and feelings and not on the opinions their parents hold.

It's important that experiences in writing and reading persuasion are not delayed until the high school years. My daughter's experience—which unfortunately is not atypical—was that in ninth or tenth grade she was expected to write persuasion, though essentially it was not taught. It was assumed that her backlog of writing experience would allow her to argue well and cogently as a ninth grader. She had difficulty. The ability to write stories or poems well does not translate immediately into writing persuasively.

TOM: Does the fact that we generally do not deal with persuasion in the elementary years indicate that we view children as essentially powerless? It seems to me that children in previous eras had greater access to persuasion—sermons and political speeches.

JACK: I think there's a sense of powerlessness that we associate with childhood, and a sense in which we don't seem to be preparing children to become citizens in a democracy, and in that way the art of persuasion is very important.

This is going off the track a bit, but so much of our politics, now, seems to work against people thinking something through, and there's a sense in which I agree with Hofstadter's portrayal of anti-intellectualism in America. Especially now, we seem to want to create followers and not thinkers. And so much of the total reading and writing experience for kids in elementary schools tends to confirm that, rather than supporting empowerment and getting them to think and reason. They're expected to follow this, do that. That's one of my primary objections to workbooks—they create that sense of following. The workbook is telling you where you are. You don't even know yourself where you are.

TOM: And you don't know how good you are. How well you're doing. You can't evaluate your own work.

JACK: That's right. But one of the things that I like about persuasive writing is that it gets students to take what is usually an emotional reaction, some change in the school that they want, and realize that they can subject that reaction to reason, to speculative thinking, and decide whether it really is an informed position that they're holding. It seems to me that this is exactly what we want to do, not only about school but about our policy toward the Middle East or any number of issues.

TOM: You recently completed a series of interviews with Katherine Paterson [author of *Bridge to Terabithia*] for Random House, over twenty-five hours in all. What were the most important things you learned from the interviews?

JACK: One of the most important things was having a writer— a working writer—define her idiosyncratic working style. We have a tendency, even with the writing process, to think that we're acknowledging all the idiosyncracies that could exist, and in the end I don't think we do. In the end I think we start to feel there ought to be certain kinds of planning you go through. There can be certain variations in revision, but basically we take a fairly narrow view. Katherine doesn't share what she's working on until she finishes the first draft—and her husband doesn't even know the subject of her work until the end of that draft. She doesn't recommend this process for anyone, but at the same time, you have her sitting in front of you, knowing that she's written ten books. As Katherine is fond of saying, "Whatever works."

These interviews reconfirmed for me how careful I have to be in working with my kids. Yes, I want them to have certain kinds of experiences, to know certain options. But in the end, it's whatever works. I had a student, a Japanese boy, two years ago, who prewrote everything in his head, and it drove me crazy. There would be nothing on paper, and then it would come out and it was excellent. It was virtually a final draft when it appeared because he was doing all this mental rehearsal. And I'm saying to Jiro, "This is really inefficient." He knows it's inefficient in a sense, because he's always the last one done. But the point is it works, and in the end I shouldn't deny that.

TOM: What experiences do teachers need to become better teachers of reading and writing? I'm thinking of in-service work.

JACK: We need to create situations where teachers are readers and writers. The next step is to make them aware of what they're going through. This awareness of our own processes is crucial because we're so good at denying our own experience, so ready to allow some expert to tell us, "This is really how you read."

I do these Martian experiments with my kids. I ask them, "How do you read a book?" Almost universally their answer is that you open it up, start at the first page, and read every word all the way through. And then you get them to talk about how they in fact read (this would be the Martian view) and it's very different. I mean, kids are opening up books in the middle. They think they're cheating and read the last page first, they look at the number of pictures and pages, they look at the chapters. They do all these things, but they deny their experience because it goes against the official word on how you read. And I think teachers, in a lot of cases, are in the same position. We've denied how we function. Instead we say, "This is the way reading and writing ought to take place," rather than being in touch with our own experiences.

Another purpose of in-service should be helping teachers define our goals. Is the end goal doing well on certain kinds of tests, getting into certain colleges? Is that what we're about? Or is our end goal to create lifelong learners? I think these different goals affect how we perceive our classrooms. My experience is that most people—especially in elementary school—look at their class in terms of what's expected the next year. So we're always in a process of preparing kids for what comes next, instead of creating experiences that are so rich that year that they'll help sustain a child for life. That's what I want for my students and for teachers.

References

Dunning, Stephen, et al. 1966. *Reflections on a Gift of Watermelon Pickle.* New York: Lothrop.

Frost, Robert. 1979. "October." In *The Poetry of Robert Frost.* New York: Holt, Rinehart and Winston.

Hofstadter, Richard. 1963. *Anti-Intellectualism in American Life.* New York: Knopf.

Paterson, Katherine. 1977. *Bridge to Terabithia.* New York: Harper and Row.

Wilde, Jack. 1985. "Play, Power, and Plausibility: The Growth of Fiction Writers." In *Breaking Ground: Teachers Relate Reading and Writing in the Elementary School,* ed. Jane Hansen, Thomas Newkirk, and Donald Graves, 121–32. Portsmouth, N.H.: Heinemann.

———. 1988. "The Written Report: Old Wine in New Bottles." In *Understanding Writing: Ways of Observing, Learning, and Teaching,* 2d ed., ed. Thomas Newkirk and Nancie Atwell, 179–90. Portsmouth, N.H.: Heinemann.

Wojciechowska, Maia. 1969. *Hey, What's Wrong with This One?* New York: Harper and Row.

WHEN LITERATURE AND WRITING MEET

DONNA SKOLNICK
Westport Public Schools
Westport, Connecticut

*L*ast April, when I walked into Karen Stafford's first-grade classroom, Becky rushed over with her work in progress. It was a fairy tale about a little girl, called Cinnamon because of her cinnamon-colored hair. Becky held her paper in front of my face.

"Look, Mrs. Skolnick," she gasped. "What I wrote sounds just like in a book." Becky read from page three of her story: "And at that she ran to get her things, but the troopers stopped her dead in her tracks."

Becky was right. Her language did sound "just like in a book." Her teacher and I exchanged glances as we celebrated Becky's discovery with her.

Becky's discovery was also my discovery. She was one of many children who showed me that being a writer is not something you grow into, like the winter coats my mother bought at the January sales. Writers of all ages share the same concerns, difficulties, and dreams. Whether I am talking about writing with adults during a writing workshop or with children in a kindergarten classroom, our conversations echo the same themes. We all strive to write "like in a book." When I read Anne Tyler and laugh out loud, I wonder "How does she do that?" Like the Little League player watching Darryl Strawberry, I want to do what my hero does.

What is the role of literature in the writing classroom? Five years ago I thought only in terms of story starters and book reports. But my own desire to write "like in a book" forced me to look more closely at the craft of the writer. Literature became my textbook: fine writing held lessons I wanted to learn.

I am the school's writing resource teacher, working in five classrooms each day. This past year, while collaborating with teachers and conferring with writers, I searched for evidence that students, too, would grow as writers when they enjoyed fine literature. In observing writers at work, listening as they talked about their writing, and interviewing them, I found my answer. What children read and how they read do influence their writing. Peter, a student in Ann Shames's first grade, expressed it this way: "My own books are longer because I've heard more books and I learned how authors write and how they put in details, and I do the same thing."

"Illuminating the craft of the writer"—these are words I first heard from my colleague, Jack McGarvey. I wrapped the phrase in a small white hankie, just as I did my milk money many years ago, and tucked it safely in the back of my mind. Since then, my experience in the classroom has given his words shape and definition. For me, they are at the heart of the reading-writing connection. When teachers illuminate the craft of the writer, students take note and begin to craft their own words.

As Mary Lou Woodruff's third-grade class read E. B. White's *Trumpet of the Swan,* she encouraged the children to notice White's vivid descriptions. Later, when she interviewed students to find out if they did anything differently in their writing because of White, Peter said, "I write stronger language, put in more detail, and tell more about the thing I am writing about." Adam commented, "Reading this book helped me to learn to expand my characters." And Elyssa offered, "I make different descriptions. I love his beautiful language." By looking at the book as a piece of writing by an author, the students added another dimension to the act of reading: learning about writing.

Mini-lessons are a natural time for teachers and children to explore the craft of the writer. I keep a large wall chart of "Tips for Writers" that lists the ones we have done. To help her second graders understand that authors choose words carefully as they write, during a mini-lesson Jane Fraser told the class: "Earlier this morning, as we shared Lilian Moore's *I'll Meet You at the Cucumbers,* I noticed that Moore used special language. Remember the way she described the truck coming down the road? 'At first he thought two small stars had tumbled out of the sky. Then he realized that what he saw were two headlights. The farmer's truck was coming down the road, home from the city.' I love the way she said that: 'two small stars had tumbled out of the sky.' Those words give me a crystal-clear image. Moore didn't say, 'He could see the lights on the truck' or just, 'He saw the truck coming down the road.' The language she chose has a special sound. As you write today, think about the words you choose. What picture do you want to give the reader? What special language will *you* try in your story today?"

Near the end of writing workshop, Katie asked if she could share her story at the group meeting. "I've used special language," she announced as she settled herself on the author's stool. She began reading her story about four mice, then paused. "This is my best part," she said. " 'He saw the biggest cheese store in the world. He got his friend. They went to the store. It was a dream to them. They were in delight they were so happy.' "

The rewards of a mini-lesson are not necessarily immediate and tangible. Incorporating new techniques into writing often throws the young writer off balance, and patience is paramount. Jane Fraser will continue to talk about special language periodically during mini-lessons, conferences, and group sharing. As students begin to notice special language in literature and in the writing of their classmates, they will experiment with it when they are ready.

What follows is a sampling of some of my own literary mini-lessons. I offer it not as a complete list of topics to be covered, but in order to demonstrate how I have used books to illuminate the author's craft. Any well-written book can illustrate similar lessons.

- Sounds:
  Ghost's Hour, Spook's Hour, Eve Bunting
- Surprise:
  The Wolf's Chicken Stew, Keiko Kasza
  Jumanji, Chris Van Allsburg
- Beautiful language:
  When I Was Young in the Mountains, Cynthia Rylant
  Owl Moon, Jane Yolen
- Story shape:
  Birthday Presents, Cynthia Rylant
  I Go with My Family to Grandma's, Riki Levinson
  Ladybug, Ladybug, Ruth Brown
- Leads:

Sarah, Plain and Tall, Patricia MacLachlan
Solomon the Rusty Nail, William Steig
From Hand to Mouth, James Cross Giblin
* Endings:
  The Man Who Wanted to Live Forever, Selina Hastings
  I'll Always Love You, Hans Wilhelm
* Dialogue:
  Wilfred Gordon McDonald Partridge, Mem Fox
  The Mother's Day Mice, Eve Bunting
* Repetition:
  The Napping House, Don and Audrey Wood
  What's Claude Doing? Dick Gackenbach
  The Relatives Came, Cynthia Rylant
* Plausibility:
  Loudmouth George and the Sixth-Grade Bully, Nancy Carlson
* Sequels:
  Willy the Wimp and *Willy the Champ,* Anthony Browne
* Variations:
  Stone Soup, Tony Ross
  Prince Cinders, Babette Cole
* Topic selection:
  Our Cat Flossie, Ruth Brown
  Minerva Louise, Janet Morgan Stoeke
* Characterization:
  My Grandson Lew, Charlotte Zolotow
* Memories into story:
  Higher on the Door, James Stevenson
  When I Was Young in the Mountains, Cynthia Rylant
* Detail:
  The Garden of Abdul Gasazi, Chris Van Allsburg
  I'll Meet You at the Cucumbers, Lilian Moore
  Beaver at Long Pond, William and Lindsay George

During the mini-lesson, I read a book aloud with a tip for writers in mind, but I know that writers will learn their own lessons, as Steven did in Sylvia Barton's kindergarten class. Before writing, the class gathered on the rug and I read *The Napping House.* I explained that the story was about the authors' son, who would only nap at his grandma's house. "Writers often use events that happen in their own lives for their stories."

The students returned to their tables to draw and write their own books. As the period ended, Steven's teacher showed me his story, a delightful account of how he played outside with his older brother. We chuckled at the way he had arranged his words—going down the page like blocks stacked in a tower—just like in *The Napping House*. That wasn't what I had meant to teach, but it was an important reminder for me: learners construct their own meaning.

A discussion topic in reading class can also become the focus of a writing mini-lesson. In Mary Lou Woodruff's third grade, readers looked through the books they were reading and developed a list of the characteristics of leads they liked. They decided that a good lead has strong feelings, detail, dialogue, action, information, and humor, that it makes use of the senses, that it makes you want to read more, and that it takes you right into the story. Mary Lou reminded her students of this list in her writing mini-lesson, and when they turned to their own writing, they thought about their leads in a fresh way. Elyssa revised her lead to read: "Everybody had something to say except me. If only Jane hadn't torn up my homework and fed it to her hamster." Tyler also reworked his lead: "When Scott woke up that Sunday, he could hear the mailman shoving the paper into the mailbox." And Kevin revised his: "You are traveling back in time. Your body particles are being separated."

When I confer with writers individually or in small clusters, I discover new opportunities to use literature to teach about writing. Peter, a third grader, asked me to listen to his story about a father and son who were walking through a forest on their way to a lake to go fishing. Peter had used specific details, but he had not included any sounds in his description. I showed him passages in Eve Bunting's *Ghost's Hour, Spook's Hour* in which she uses sound words. Leah, listening in, showed Peter where she had written about "the leaves crunching under their feet" in her own story. When I gave the book to Peter, inviting him to enjoy Bunting's story, he looked me in the eye. "Writing a story's hard work," he said. "Writing a *good* story is hard work," I replied. "You no longer want just to write a story. You want to craft your words to make your story the best you can." I congratulated Peter and moved on to confer with another writer. One of the best ways to illustrate an abstract writing tip is to point out a concrete example, which is why a literary environment, full of fine books, is an essential resource for teaching writing.

Group share is another time when discussion focuses on the writer's craft—of both student and professional authors. During group share, students learn to recognize and celebrate the developing craft of their fellow authors. Jessica's story impressed her classmates with its lyrical lead:

> At night when the crickets were chirping and the stars were out and everything was stirring in the wind, down, down, down, below the sky, below the earth, below the root, lay the Ringle family, fast asleep.

When she finished reading her piece, whispers circled the room—"Wow, that's good!"—and creative wheels started to turn. Knowing that another eight-year-old can craft such vivid writing inspired others to give it a go.

When Mary Lou Woodruff interviewed her third graders at the end of the year to find out what had helped them most in writing workshop, over three-quarters of the children mentioned group share. Elyssa said, "When everybody shares you get ideas for writing." Jonathan added, "You get the chance to talk about good writing." And Leah explained, "Listening to good stories made me want to express my feelings and share with others. Going through the experience of watching everyone write, and conferring, and talking about writing and reading, helps."

One day in May I asked Andrew, a third grader new to the school, to compare his writing experience in his new class to that of his previous one. "It's easier to write in here," he said. "We have more time. The kids seem to know so much more about writing, too. I don't think the kids in my old class even knew what a good lead is." When I asked what his new teacher did differently, he responded with conviction: "My other teacher never sat us down and talked about writing. She never talked about suspense in a story, dialogue, leads, and stuff like that. She just had us write." Andrew learned quickly that writers need to talk about their own writing with other writers. Literary discussion—during mini-lessons, conferences, and group share —elevates the quality of children's writing and deepens children's understanding of writing as a craft. But this understanding will only grow if the classroom soil is enriched by conversations about writing: good writing teachers are familiar with interesting and exciting books and know how to talk about them.

Writing workshop is a literary event. My role is to be the senior reader and writer, to show students that I value and celebrate literature in my own life. When I find a memorable passage in a book I'm reading, I read it aloud in a mini-lesson. As I confer with students, I watch for connections. I often hear myself say, "That reminds me of another story. Have you read . . . ?" Or, "Be sure to share this with Peter. Your story reminds me of one he wrote." In this way, I work to interweave literature and writing. Then, as students confer, they begin to forge their own connections—to the writing of others and to the books they have read. Before long, every child is able to enjoy writing and to write well. When students see a book as a piece of writing, conceived and crafted by a fellow author, they begin to see themselves as writers, learning and practicing their craft.

References

Brown, Ruth. 1986. *Our Cat Flossie*. New York: E. P. Dutton.

———. 1988. *Ladybug, Ladybug*. New York: E. P. Dutton.

Browne, Anthony. 1985. *Willy the Wimp*. New York: Alfred A. Knopf.

———. 1986. *Willy the Champ*. New York: Alfred A. Knopf.

Bunting, Eve. 1986. *The Mother's Day Mice*. New York: Clarion Books.

———. 1987. *Ghost's Hour, Spook's Hour*. New York: Clarion Books.

Carlson, Nancy. 1983. *Loudmouth George and the Sixth-Grade Bully*. New York: Puffin Books.

Cole, Babette. 1987. *Prince Cinders*. New York: G. P. Putnam's Sons.

Fox, Mem. 1985. *Wilfred Gordon McDonald Partridge*. New York: Kane/Miller Books.

Gackenbach, Dick. 1984. *What's Claude Doing?* New York: Clarion Books.

George, William T., and Lindsay Barrett George. 1988. *Beaver at Long Pond*. New York: Greenwillow Books.

Giblin, James Cross. 1987. *From Hand to Mouth*. New York: Thomas Y. Crowell.

Hastings, Selina. 1988. *The Man Who Wanted to Live Forever*. New York: Henry Holt.

Kasza, Keiko. 1987. *The Wolf's Chicken Stew*. New York: G. P. Putnam's Sons.

Levinson, Riki. 1986. *I Go with My Family to Grandma's*. New York: E. P. Dutton.

MacLachlan, Patricia. 1985. *Sarah, Plain and Tall*. New York: Harper & Row.

Moore, Lilian. 1988. *I'll Meet You at the Cucumbers*. New York: Atheneum.

Ross, Tony. 1987. *Stone Soup*. New York: Dial Books.

Rylant, Cynthia. 1982. *When I Was Young in the Mountains*. New York: E. P. Dutton.

———. 1985. *The Relatives Came*. New York: Bradbury Press.

———. 1987. *Birthday Presents*. New York: Orchard Books.

Steig, William. 1985. *Solomon the Rusty Nail*. New York: Farrar, Straus & Giroux.

Stevenson, James. 1987. *Higher on the Door*. New York: Greenwillow Books.

Stoeke, Janet Morgan. 1988. *Minerva Louise*. New York: E. P. Dutton.

Van Allsburg, Chris. 1979. *The Garden of Abdul Gasazi*. Boston: Houghton Mifflin.

————. 1981. *Jumanji*. Boston: Houghton Mifflin.

White, E.B. 1973. *The Trumpet of the Swan*. New York: Harper & Row.

Wilhelm, Hans. 1985. *I'll Always Love You*. New York: Crown Publishers.

Wood, Audrey. 1984. *The Napping House*. New York: Harcourt Brace Jovanovich.

Yolen, Jane. 1987. *Owl Moon*. New York: Philomel Books.

Zolotow, Charlotte. 1974. *My Grandson Lew*. New York: Harper & Row.

A GARDEN OF POETS

CORA FIVE
Edgewood School
Scarsdale, New York

*I*n contrast to summers past, when former students mailed me stories about their summer adventures, the letter I received from Christie was a poem.

> Dear Miss Five,
>
>> Flash of yellow
>> Nothing.
>> A loud clap, as yellow touches ground
>> in a crooked, jagged line.
>> A scream.
>> Quiet.
>
>> Love,
>> Christie
>
> P. S. Can you guess what my image was?

Christie's poem had particular significance for me. In my first eight years as a teacher of writing, my students did not write poetry because I was afraid to teach it. I remembered struggling through high school and college lit courses, analyzing poems and writing papers that compared the works of major poets born hundreds of years ago. This past year, despite my insecurity, I finally decided to expose my fifth graders to poetry and see what happened.

During the summer I had heard Nancie Atwell speak about using poetry in the classroom. She had suggested that teachers read poetry aloud to their kids, but only poems that they truly enjoyed. Before school started I bought poetry collections edited or written by X. J. Kennedy, Lee Bennett Hopkins, Robert Frost,

61

and Myra Cohn Livingston. I began to read and—for perhaps the first time in my life—I started to enjoy poetry. At a conference that fall I heard Kennedy and Hopkins read their work. I was entranced. I practiced reading their poetry the way they had read it. I told my class about these poets and their readings, and how much I liked their work. And then I began to read the poems aloud. The kids liked them!

The next day I read more. The poems I selected were short, funny, and about everyday experiences. I took samples from *Brats* (1968) and *The Forgetful Wishing Well* (1985) by Kennedy and *Dinosaurs* (1987a) by Hopkins, which I kept in the classroom. After I read the poems, I showed copies on the overhead projector so my students could see the form of each poem. Sometimes they made comments about the poetry, but often they were silent as they thought about what they had heard. Adhering to Hopkins's (1987b) recommendation, I did not pose any comprehension questions or ask whether and why students liked the poems. We just sat silently and savored.

Following another of Atwell's suggestions (1987), I made copies of the poems I read available so kids could have copies of the poems they liked to keep in special folders for rereading and sharing. I also began to tape favorite poems on the walls, between the windows, and on the doors of the classroom.

After I had read funny poems, I turned to an anthology compiled by X. J. and Dorothy M. Kennedy called *Knock at a Star* (1982), which contains a number of different kinds of poetry and gives brief information about each type. I began reading poems to the children from various categories in the section titled "What Poems Do." When I realized that the kids looked forward to these readings, I began to spend more time reading and selecting poems on my own. I noticed, too, that students were choosing poetry books to read during reading workshop. Poetry gradually began to spread throughout my community of readers. Once a few children started reading and sharing poems, others began to select the same titles, first books of poetry I kept in the classroom, then books from the poetry shelves of the library. Shel Silverstein's *A Light in the Attic* (1981) and *Where the Sidewalk Ends* (1974) and Jack Prelutsky's *The New Kid on the Block* (1984) were popular titles in the beginning. Some children chose to read favorite poems at our sharing time at the end of reading workshop. Again, kids responded freely and I often joined in. I never suggested that they write poetry during writing workshop.

Then, in January, we had a snow day and the next morning I received a surprise. Naomi came rushing into school to tell me she had written some poems about snow and read her favorite to the class. It was a rhyming poem describing the first snowstorm and the activities made possible by the snow.

Snow
by Naomi

> Snow, snow
> you need a shovel
> instead of a hoe.
> Whirling, twirling
> in the air,
> there's white stuff everywhere!
> Telephone rings
> ding-ety ding.
> It makes me want to sing.
> No school today
> Hip, hip hurray!
> I've got a plan
> let's make a snowman!
> There's two inches on the ground.
> We heard every sound,
> A cat's meow
> and a plow!
> No joggers today
> They're having a holiday.
> Radio says cars are stuck.
> What luck
> is on my side today.

She told me she had written about the snow in poem form because "you've been reading all those poems to us." I was delighted. In a group share, many of the boys said they wanted to write a poem like Naomi's. They especially liked the way the words rhymed. I thought about their comments. Even though I had read many kinds of poems, including free verse, students still felt that poems had to rhyme or enjoyed the genre because of the rhyme.

Brendan surprised me next with a story poem he wrote during writing workshop. I had read story poems to the class the previous week. He was excited when he came to share during a group conference. "This is the story of a troublemaker named Billy," he said.

Billy Is Going West

by Brendan

Do you know what Billy did?
Guess?
He traveled all the way
across the U.S.
He started in Maine
and advanced West.
And every state has got
a warrant for his arrest.

In D.C. he made a crank call
to Ronnie.
doing his imitation of
Mikhail Gorbie.

He said he was planning
to drop the bomb
and the old U.S.A.
would surely be gone.

In Miami he went on
the set of "Miami Vice"
and got caught playing with
Crocket's alligator twice.

In the Alamo he started
a big, huge mess.
He tried to set fire to
the tour guide's dress.

In California he went
to the beach
so he could sit
in the lifeguard's seat.

But instead of acting nice
the rest of the day,
he took the lifeguard's
whistle away.

They threw him off the beach
and said he was insane!
So old Billy went
all the way back to Maine.

Do you know what Billy did?
Guess?
He traveled all the way
across the U.S.
He started in Maine
and advanced West

And every other state has got
a warrant for his arrest.

Brendan not only remembered the pattern of some of the story poems I had read, he also used the technique of repeated lines and verses he had heard in other poems.

During our study of American history, the class was involved in writing about aspects of colonial life and the Revolution. I played a recording of Longfellow's poem "The Midnight Ride of Paul Revere." Jennifer, who was writing a report on Paul Revere, decided to try a poem.

The Famous Ride of Paul Revere
by Jennifer

On Tuesday night
when the moon was full,
two lanterns hung
from a window sill,
and without giving
any pain,
Paul Revere dug his spurs
and pulled his reins.

Over the hills
up and down,
through every little
village and town,
because this was Revere's
famous ride,
he rode on with great pride.

But Paul Revere
was in a hurry,
so he cried his alarm
and the people would scurry.
But never fear,
the minutemen are here,
so on rode
the famous Paul Revère!

The kids and I were enthusiastic about the poems Brendan and Jennifer had written. When they finished reading, the room was filled with animated conversation, and I was amazed at the support these kids received as they experimented with this "new" genre. Suddenly everyone was interested in writing poetry as well as reading it, and I wondered who would try a poem next. Christie, a shy, quiet girl, took the risk and wrote a rhyming poem on raindrops. Again, the class responded to the rhyme, and I began to wonder why rhyme seemed to be an easier, safer way for these ten-year-olds to write poetry. Perhaps it provided a structure or perhaps it seemed more natural for poetry to have a rhythm or a beat. Whatever the reason, they were having fun with their rhyming verse, and their enthusiasm was infectious.

At this point I still had not conducted a formal lesson on the writing of poetry. Instead, I continued to observe what would happen if I let the class go at its own pace. Because I knew I did not want to force all my fifth graders to write poetry at the same time in a group lesson, I continued to read poetry aloud —poetry that described feelings, settings, or characters by Frost, Hughes, Livingston—and students continued to share poems that they liked. I read poetry for myself, and I read to find poems to read to the class. In the process I became very involved in the genre. I discovered poems I loved, reread often, and wanted to share. I began to worry that there wouldn't be enough time to read them all.

In the middle of January, I introduced similes in a formal way in a series of reading mini-lessons. Following a suggestion by Stewig (1980), I used the filmstrip and recording of a book called *A Picture Has a Special Look* by Helen Borten (1961), which describes different art materials through similes. I showed the filmstrip twice, and the children began to pick out the similes, remarking on the ones they especially liked. After the filmstrip, the class tried out similes of their own: "as ecstatic as the Giants winning the Superbowl," "as conspicuous as an evergreen in the desert," "as prominent as a royal king," "as desolate as a hermit," "melancholy like a child who lost his only dime." For the next few days my students described everything in similes.

The following week we talked about metaphors. I read Rowena Bennett's "A Modern Dragon" from *The Sound of Poetry* (1967), "Metaphor" from Merriam's *It Doesn't Always Have to Rhyme* (1964), and Vachel Lindsay's "The Moon's the North Wind's Cooky" from *Piping Down the Valleys Wild* (1968) and again, after a few days, students were eager to write their own. Jeremy modeled his first metaphor, which he did not consider a poem, on "A Modern Dragon."

The Garbage Dragon

A garbage truck is a dragon
with a giant mouth that chews up food.
And when it turns backwards

its two eyes brighten up at night.
When it gets to the garbage dump
it is a dragon feeding its young.

Jennifer wrote about fire:

Fire

Fire is a devil
that shimmers and glows.
It can rise to the ceiling
or go down to one coal.

They were off again. Now they wrote and spoke in metaphors.
"The Constitution is peace on paper," said Brendan. "The rain
is a jovial person crying sobs of joy," Jeremy told me one rainy
morning. And I found myself thinking and speaking in similes
and metaphors, too.

My students discovered metaphors in the trade books they
were reading and exclaimed in delight when they heard them
in the books I read aloud. Jeremy sighed one day as he worked
on a math problem and then blurted out, "I look out the window
and I don't just see trees and snow. I see metaphors!"

And then, in February, Dayna wrote a metaphor that gradually grew into a poem describing the color black.

The Color Black
by Dayna

The color black is a still isolated flower
on top of a lonely hill.
It can not be seen
and can not be heard.
Black is final like the end of a sunset.
Black is strong and solid.
It has no meaning
It has no words.
Black can be found anywhere,
at the bottom of empty holes
or when the lights are turned off.
Black can make your eyes feeble
like a newborn baby trying to lift his head.
Black is a cub that has to leave his mother
to go into the wilderness.
Black might be a beginning
or an ending.

The class and I were stunned at the depth of Dayna's poem.
Students responded to her imagery, to the way she used similes

and metaphors to create meaning. Through their discussion of her poem, they began to see the possibilities available to them in writing poetry.

Dayna's poem marked a turning point in my class. It seemed to free the rest of the kids, and they began to use poetry to express their feelings, their fears, and their thoughts. Their reliance on rhyme decreased. Their poetry got better and better. Beautiful language seemed to flow out of them and they marveled at the results, often saying, "I can't believe I wrote this."

Jeremy, who expressed concern about death, wrote:

Light and Dark   Life and Death

There is a place that is as dark as a lion's throat.
In this place no trees or plants dare to grow
and no animals dare to live.
This place is like a funeral for a loved one.
It is the disappearance of your favorite pet.
This place is death.

There is also a place as light as the reflection
of the sun off a stained glass window,
The place is the sound of a wave
crashing against the side of a rock.
It is as bright as birth
or saving someone.
This place is life.

Once again, there was an enthusiastic response, but now the kids were interested in the ideas—the meaning Jeremy presented and the images he used. As with Dayna's poem, they discussed each line and wondered how the descriptions had come to him. There was no talk about the lack of rhyme.

Then Jasmina, who came to our school two years ago from Yugoslavia, wrote a poem about music.

Music

Music, like the loud roar
of the wild sea
as it comes upon a helpless ship.

Music, like the soft humming
of the leaves on the trees
as a gentle breeze slowly goes by.

Music, like a stern, harsh voice
telling you what to do
or the tapping of the people's feet
as they walk hurriedly by.

Music, like a story in a book,
a feeling of sorrow and doom
that a wild horse of the desert feels
when it realizes it cannot get free of its enemy.

Music, like the color black
rhyming with white
as in a starry night.

Music is everything
I imagine it to be,
as the wind of the North
carries different tones, colors, and feelings
through my soul.

By March, poetry had become important not only in the read-ing and writing program but in the total classroom environment. It appeared in all areas of the curriculum. I marveled at the ease with which my kids wrote verses, shared, conferred, and made decisions about revision. They decided, either individually or together, when a poem was finished, and they read their com-pleted poems with pride and pleasure. How did poetry become so special to these fifth graders? I think many factors contributed to the successful integration of poetry into the reading and writ-ing program.

First and most important, I made a personal investment in poetry. I began to read it and enjoy it, and I brought my en-thusiasm and joy to the kids as I shared the poems I loved. They, in turn, began to share poems they loved. We ventured together into the world of poetry, first through reading and then through writing. Reading lots of poetry aloud took time. But just as I had learned the importance of reading aloud to my class each day to encourage their interest in reading, I found that reading poetry aloud was the impetus for students to read and write poems themselves.

The classroom environment was another important factor. Students worked as a community of readers and writers. In writing workshop they supported and encouraged each other. Through talking they learned from each other, and took ad-vantage of many opportunities to respond and share ideas. Be-cause I did not "teach" poetry, students did not feel that there was one correct way to write it. I exposed them to many kinds of poems and highlighted poetic features in my mini-lessons, but I did not force them to write poetry. They wrote when they were ready. They used published authors and, especially, each other as models, and they felt free to experiment with different techniques, images, and vocabulary. Those who started writing poetry in the winter shared their processes and encouraged students who were still reluctant to try. The writing of poetry eventually spread throughout my community of writers. As they became more confident in the medium, they were willing to leave rhyme behind and take risks with meaning and feelings. Poetry allowed my students to be playful and to express their deepest thoughts, and it added a wonderful new dimension to my reading program. More important, it became a source of pleasure and awe for all of us. Jennifer's poem, written at the end of the year, best describes the growth of my fifth-grade poets.

The Garden of Writers
by Jennifer

> In the beginning of the year
> we were all a seed.
> When we were put into the ground
> it was the same as being put
> into Miss Five's class.
> Her teachings were like the water
> and the sunlight.
> And the flowers grew.
>
> Some of us were snow flowers
> We bloomed in winter.
> Others were crocuses
> We bloomed in early spring.
> The rest were tulips
> blooming in April and May.
> Now, right before the end of the year,
> Miss Five has a beautiful garden.

References

Atwell, N. 1987. *In the Middle: Writing, Reading, and Learning with Adolescents.* Portsmouth, N.H.: Boynton/Cook.

Bennett, R. 1967. "A Modern Dragon." In *The Sound of Poetry*, ed. M. C. Austin and A. B. Mills. Boston: Allyn and Bacon.

Borten, H. 1961. *A Picture Has a Special Look.* New York: Abelard-Schuman (Weston Woods LTR-054).

Hopkins, L. B. 1987a. *Dinosaurs.* New York: Harcourt Brace Jovanovich.

———. 1987b. *Pass the Poetry, Please!* New York: Harper & Row.

Kennedy, X. J. 1968. *Brats.* New York: Atheneum.

———. 1985. *The Forgetful Wishing Well.* New York: Atheneum.

Kennedy, X. J., and D. M. Kennedy. 1982. *Knock at a Star.* Boston: Little, Brown and Company.

Lindsay, V. 1968. "The Moon's the North Wind's Cooky." In *Piping Down the Valleys Wild*, ed. N. Larrick. New York: Dell.

Merriam, E. 1964. *It Doesn't Always Have to Rhyme*. New York: Atheneum.

Prelutsky, J. 1984. *The New Kid on the Block*. New York: Greenwillow Books.

Silverstein, S. 1974. *Where the Sidewalk Ends*. New York: Harper & Row.

————. 1981. *A Light in the Attic*. New York: Harper & Row.

Stewig, J. W. 1980. *Read to Write*. New York: Richard C. Owen.

EVERYDAY POETS: RECOGNIZING POETRY IN PROSE

MARNA BUNCE
Crocker Farm Elementary School
Amherst, Massachusetts

S hadows lope along the mountain's rumpled flanks; they elongate like root tips, like lobes of spilling water, faster and faster. A warm purple pigment pools in each ruck and tuck of the rock; it deepens and spreads, boring crevasses, canyons.

Annie Dillard

Poetry abounds in Annie Dillard's *Pilgrim at Tinker Creek*, as it does in so many well-written books. Although some writers are more masterful than others, I seldom read a book that doesn't have at least a few lines that can be transposed as poetry.

I used to isolate my poetry units, setting aside all reading and writing of prose to concentrate on poetry, as though they were two separate entities. Neither I nor my students made any connection between the two. Invariably, several students would grumble, "Do we have to write poetry again? Can't I work on my story?" Through the years I have come to realize that poetry and prose are not disjointed genres. How we view them is important to how we teach them.

As I discovered poetry in prose, even short phrases, I began to point them out to my students. *The Wind in the Willows* by Kenneth Grahame is filled with poetic phrases: "Nature was deep in her annual slumber and seemed to have kicked the clothes off" (57) or "a mere blank transparency on the night" (86).

Another source of beautiful language is *Song of the Trees* by Mildred D. Taylor (1975), who lets us see the morning through Cassie's eyes. "I opened the window and looked outside. The earth was draped in a cloak of gray mist as the sun chased the night away" (7).

My biggest surprise, however, was discovering that children's picture books are a unique source of poetry. As Jane Yolen (1983) explains it:

> Because picture books are so small, each word must count. No sloppiness of diction, no stray adjectives, no extra ideas. A picture book is really a kind of poem and should be treated as such. (23)

Maurice Sendak's *Where the Wild Things Are* (1963), *Fox's Dream* by Keizaburo Tejima (1985), and *Dream Child* by David McPhail (1985) are excellent examples of prose-poetry, as are Byrd Baylor's *Before You Came This Way* (1969), *The Other Way to Listen* (1978), and *I'm in Charge of Celebrations* (1986). In *Owl Moon*, written by Jane Yolen and illustrated by John Schoenherr (1987), both the words and the form are poetic:

> It was late one winter night,
> long past my bedtime,
> when Pa and I went owling,
> There was no wind.
> The trees stood still
> as giant statues.
> And the moon was so bright
> the sky seemed to shine.
> Somewhere behind us
> a train whistle blew,
> long and low,
> like a sad, sad song.

The precision and rhythm of the language, the use of the white space on the page, and the format all say: poetry. Yolen's writing is filled with images that cause the reader to feel, think, reminisce.

Another book I use is *Canoeing* (1986), in which Laurie Lattig-Ehlers invites reader and listener to participate in the experience of canoeing by using sensory words: "The low sun shines hot on our backs, but the water's coolness drifts up to meet us" or "The paddles dip-splash in the water and we pull away."

If so many picture books are a form of poetry, what is poetry? I am enlightened by my students' answers:

> Poetry is a piece of writing that takes me somewhere else.

> It sets a mood, it expresses feelings, it flows.

A poem can change my mood. I read a sad poem and cry, and then a happy or funny poem and laugh.

Poetry explains something well. It makes the subject seem real.

A poem has more meaning than is on the page.

As Donald Murray states (1986), "poets are masters of precision. . . . The good poet—and the good writer in any form—does not command a reaction to the writing; the writer creates the reaction by giving the reader information that causes the reader to think or feel. Poets remind us not to preach, but merely to reveal" (427). I want my students to experience the power and beauty of poetic language.

I have used picture books for several years now as a main source for my prose mini-lessons and find them an excellent resource for any age. Since they are as long as the stories that most children write, they easily lend themselves to teaching such techniques as leads, endings, and character development. So why not poetry, too?

Discussing such literary techniques as alliteration, in prose as well as poetry, removes the mystique from poetry that turns some students away. For example, in *The Wind in the Willows* there is natural alliteration: "There's a sort of dell down here in front of us, where the ground seems all hilly and humpy and hummocky" (65). Knowledge like this can make the writing of poetry more accessible, and acceptable, to beginning writers like ten-year-old Jason:

Spring Is Here
    The warm sun glows as the green grass grows.
    Dull colors of crippled leaves show from the fall.
    Birds build nests from way up top,
    While below sap oozes from the trees.
    The wind blows calmly as bugs fly.
    Spring is here.
    Die, winter, die.

Jason did not say, "I think I'll use alliteration in this poem." I had pointed out examples of alliteration in mini-lessons on prose and poetry, and Jason had obviously internalized the technique. In his self-evaluation Jason explained, "I made this poem when we went outside and made notes. When the notes were done, I rearranged the sentences so that they made sense. Then I added and took away words. Next I circled sentences that I liked to put in the poem, and finally I was ready for my final copy."

This brings me to another discovery that stems from a suggestion made by Kathy Anderson, a poet-in-residence in my classroom. Kathy believes that children should be able to borrow words they like from poems she reads to them and use these words in their own poetry. I followed her suggestion and realized its value. It encourages children to create a personal thesaurus, a treasury of words they might never have thought of—fresh words that they can easily retrieve later and use as models. I often overhear children sharing their lists with each other as they search for the "perfect" word.

Rachel had written the words *fawn* and *doe* in her thesaurus. These words gave her an idea. "The rest of the poem," she said, "just came to me." Rachel wrote:

> I watched a fawn grow
> into a doe
> yesterday.
> I felt myself turn
> from eight
> to eight and a half.

Nine-year-old Kate had collected the words *fox, vanish, aching pains, yelping, mountain,* and *heaven* from various examples of prose and poetry that we had read together in the classroom. We had just finished a unit on animals of New England when she composed this poem.

The Fox

> The mother fox climbed the mountain
> knowing she would die soon.
> She brought her babies
> to her best friend's house.
>
> She left her poor cubs with her.
> Her heart was in pain,
> leaving her cubs,
> but she would die anyway.
>
> She walked to the top of the mountain
> and fell to the ground.
> Her cubs had gotten away
> and came yelping after her.
>
> Her body vanished.
> She was now in the heaven of sky
> with all the other animals.

The cubs saw her body on a cloud
and knew she was happy.
But they had aching pains
in their little hearts.

Both the prose and poetry I had shared in class and Kate's thesaurus, which gave her a concrete way to keep some of the words she had heard, helped shape the mood she created and the words she used in her poem.

Another day I used "Poem" by Langston Hughes (1960) as part of a mini-lesson on the "shapes" of poems.

Poem

I loved my friend.
He went away from me.
There is nothing more to say.
The poem ends,
Soft as it began—
I loved my friend.

As I read "Poem," I showed it on the overhead projector in large print because I want the children to see the poem's shape, which is part of its essence. Eleven-year-old Job asked if he could borrow a copy and with it in hand, disappeared into a corner of the room. A little while later he reappeared with this:

So long ago we had the best of times.
We did so much, but at the same time
so little. If it were possible I'd
do it all over again.

The poem is about Job and his best friend, who had moved away two years earlier. Langston Hughes's words brought back feelings of happy hours mixed with loneliness and gave Job a way to express those same feelings.

Poet Sheila Cowing (1987) writes,

Why a poem and not a story? Because a poem seems so well suited for feeling, for making it happen on a page. A poem, using the tools of our five senses, makes pictures of a memory, a dream, a past experience, even something that may be as fleeting as a feeling. It catches the essence of a person. (59)

Chris caught the essence of an experience in his poem "The Cookie Jar." He enjoyed the carefree way Arnold Adoff expressed his thoughts in *Eats* (1979) and tried Adoff's techniques himself.

The Cookie Jar

> There it is
> > sitting
> on the counter
> > > looking
> > so innocent.
> I shouldn't take
> > the plunge,
> but I do.
> > > There is nothing there.

Arnold Adoff was Chris's model for this poem, as Langston Hughes was for Job's. The next time, their models might be Valerie Worth, Ann Turner, or William Carlos Williams. So many poets with so many styles—we need only expose our children to their works. Keeping a variety of poetry books on display in our classrooms makes the work of these poets available for mini-lessons and for individual enjoyment.

In writing workshop I often find myself pointing out lines from a particular poem to a child who is stuck for an idea or an effect and suggesting that the child see how another writer handled the same problem. Then I walk away. When I return, more often than not, the child has solved the writing problem. Seeing how words are put together on a page shows children so clearly what all my rhetoric cannot, and the fresh language and imagery help them verbalize their own observations, thoughts, and feelings.

If poetry is to become a natural part of our students' lives, they need to see it, listen to it, say it, write it, and collect it. They need to own copies of the poems they really like. I ask children to search through a variety of poetry books for poems that demonstrate the techniques I have discussed in mini-lessons, poems that elicit certain feelings, and poems that are their favorites. Then I photocopy them so that children can have their own personal anthologies.

Poetry is not meant to be considered in isolation. The elements of poetry infuse our speaking and our writing, and we need to help our students see the connection. Recognizing the poetry in prose, learning new words, and hearing their own and other voices—these are ways children connect their thoughts and feelings to the world of language.

References

Adoff, Arnold. 1979. *Eats*. New York: Lothrop, Lee & Shepard Books.

Baylor, Byrd. 1969. *Before You Came This Way*. New York: E.P. Dutton.

————. 1978. *The Other Way to Listen*. New York: Charles Scribner's Sons.

————. 1986. *I'm in Charge of Celebrations*. New York: Charles Scribner's Sons.

Cowing, Sheila. 1987. "Why a Poem and Not a Story." *Shoe Tree* 3 (Fall): 59.

Dillard, Annie. 1974. *Pilgrim at Tinker Creek*. New York: Harper's Magazine Press.

Grahame, Kenneth. 1969. *The Wind in the Willows*. New York: New American Library.

Hughes, Langston. 1960. "Poem," in *Don't You Turn Back*. New York: Alfred A. Knopf.

Lattig-Ehlers, Laurie. 1986. *Canoeing*. Natick, Mass.: Picture Book Studio.

McPhail, David. 1985. *Dream Child*. New York: E. P. Dutton.

Murray, Donald M. 1986. *Read to Write*. New York: Holt, Rinehart and Winston.

Sendak, Maurice. 1963. *Where the Wild Things Are*. New York: Harper & Row.

Taylor, Mildred D. 1975. *Song of the Trees*. New York: Dial Press.

Tejima, Keizaburo. 1985. *Fox's Dream*. New York: Philomel Books.

Yolen, Jane. 1983. *Writing Books for Children*. Boston: The Writer.

————. 1987. *Owl Moon*. New York: Philomel Books.

FROM PERSONAL NARRATIVE TO FICTION

KATHLEEN A. MOORE
Thorncliffe Park Elementary School
East York Board of Education
Toronto, Ontario

*T*he trees around Mouse were sparkling with rainbow colors. Mouse was deep inside the magic forest. He wondered if something magical would happen to him. He was only a very little mouse but he began to feel very, very special.

From Sanja's "The Magic Forest"

When Sanja sits on the sharing stool for a group conference, the students and I wait expectantly. We know her words will create new worlds for us to explore and enjoy. Sanja is an eight-year-old writer in my class. What could she teach me about young writers and fiction? I interviewed her to find out.

"Sanja, why did you write *The Magic Forest*?"

"I wrote it because nobody wrote fiction in this class and I wanted people to listen up to my story."

"Where did you get the idea?"

"I was reading Bill Peet's book *Huge Harold* when I got the idea of making characters more special and giving them a part to play. It's not that I wanted to write *that* particular story, but it gave me ideas for later on."

"Do you like writing fiction?"

"I love it. You can put a mole going to school to learn something, but in a true story you can't do that. Because it's from your own mind, you can do anything you want. In your mind, you can have a happy face even if you're sad and it can go in your story."

"What kind of books do you enjoy reading?"

"Sometimes I like reading true stories, but really I like fiction because I can imagine. I get more into the story. Real just doesn't go into my kind of place."

Sanja finds freedom and a sense of her real self in reading and writing fiction. She uses what she reads to give her ideas about what to write. As a writer, she finds that fiction provides a more viable vehicle for her own thoughts and feelings than does personal narrative.

Except for Sanja, none of the other twenty-six second and third graders in my class were writing fiction, and by March, I wondered why. I wanted to encourage them to try fiction, a new genre for them, while maintaining the supportive and productive atmosphere of our writing workshop. Freedom to choose their own topics, time to write, and opportunities to confer were well-established with my students. During reading time, which was also organized as a workshop, they read books of their own choosing and responded to them in journals. In addition, each day, five or six students shared what they were reading with the whole group. By March, the children had read three thousand books—joke books, alphabet books, students' published books, and trade books—of which perhaps two thousand were fiction. I was curious. Why were they still writing about sleeping at their cousin's house or visiting the mall? Lucy Calkins's comment (1986) that "fiction is what children read and it should be part of what they write" (318) began to haunt me. It was true that my students wrote longer, more interesting stories about themselves than they had in September, but I was concerned that the richness of their reading was not obvious in the stories they wrote. I wondered if I was right to expect a spontaneous transfer from students' reading to their writing or if I should nudge them into trying fiction.

Inspired by Sanja's positive view of the value of fiction, I planned a new writing occasion for my students. We began with what we knew: the reading of fiction. I asked them to read a fiction book of their own choice with a friend and gave them this instruction: "I remember times you've told me about 'falling into a story' and about being 'grabbed' by the author. Those were interesting ideas. You seemed to be saying that authors have ways of catching your interest. In the book you read this morning, try to find out what that author does to grab your attention. What 'works' in the book you read?"

My students wrote this research question at the top of a new page in their reading journals. Then they spent the rest of that Friday morning reading, talking, and making notes. In the af-

ternoon we gathered together to list their findings. I took down
their dictation on chart paper.

What Worked in the Book?

* a surprise *(Where the Wild Things Are)*
* a reversal *(Sloan and Philamina or How to Make Friends with Your Lunch)*
* always something happening *(Sadie and the Snowman)*
* someone who keeps trying *(Can I Keep Him?)*
* an animal like a person the author knows *(The Story of Ferdinand)*
* something funny *(Curious George)*
* several strange things *(We Can't Sleep)*
* made something in nature a friendly person *(Millicent and the Wind)*
* changes the usual way of things *(Jonathan Cleaned Up—Then He Heard a Sound)*
* not a happy ending or a surprise ending *(The Miller, the Son and the Donkey)*
* made you curious *(Alistair in Outer Space)*
* an unusual person *(Amelia Bedelia)*
* pattern of events happening, the beginning always comes again *(Scat! Scat!)*
* a character we liked *(Nate the Great)*
* a character we felt sorry for *(The Velveteen Rabbit)*
* a character we felt angry with *(Hansel and Gretel)*

In the classroom that afternoon I looked over their list and
wondered aloud if these stories and authors could help them
with their own fiction writing. For me, this was a change of
direction. I had always tried to lead from behind, to allow students to find their own paths of expression. Now I was going to
steer more deliberately, more of a push than a nudge, to help
them become writers of fiction. But I had some hunches, based
on my previous experiences as a reader, writer, and teacher,
about the central role of good literature in demonstrating what
authors do.

When I first read the work of John Updike in the *New Yorker*,
I was startled and attracted by the exactness and spareness of
his descriptions. I wanted to read more, and in my own writing,
I tried to see and describe life with his sharp vision. In the same
way, Lucy Calkins, Don Graves, and Nancie Atwell, through their
sensitivity and honesty, convinced me of the credibility of their
ideas, so that in my own teaching, I found that I tried to see and
describe my students with the same attitude of respect. Now,
when a wave of Robert Munsch reading rolls over my class, I
realize that his realistic depiction of childhood speaks to my

students. I observe their growing appreciation of the power of language as they trade books like baseball cards. Literature joins experience to become a new source of knowing.

The day after their reading and research on fiction, my students made special fiction folders. Each folder contained a blank sheet for planning, lined sheets for writing, and a goals sheet. Students selected items from our list of observations on what had worked in the books they had read and made these observations the goals for their own fiction. George wanted to include in his story a surprise and a pattern of events. Chirag chose to write about a change in the usual way things happen and to include something to make a reader curious. Nikhil decided to create someone who keeps trying, an unhappy ending, and a character one would be angry with. Sanja planned to write about a reversal and include a character one felt sorry for and something strange.

Before they began to write, we met at the front to review their plans. I talked again about how successful fiction writers often begin with the commonplace before luring the reader into their tales of invention and that, along the way, they use specific details to convince the reader that the story is true. My students knew this already from our book talks but had not tried it themselves in their own writing. They knew they were taking a chance but as with all their other first attempts, they also knew nobody would be breathing down their necks, challenging their ownership before the authors themselves had signed the lease.

They began to draft—or at least some did. Others drew pictures, doodled, mapped a plot, or outlined a main character. At the end of writing time, they filed their stories in their folders. It was understood that I would not read what they had written. The next day before writing workshop they met to tell me their topics; at this stage it was much too early for titles. Then they wrote again. And again the next day. Some began to have peer conferences. They met shyly in private corners to share, comment, and question. Slips of paper with ideas for changes were exchanged and stapled to rough drafts.

By the third day, amid growing curiosity about what everyone was writing, I scheduled a read-around. The students sat in a circle, their stories on the floor in front of them, and read aloud in turn what they had written so far. No author refused to read or made any apologies, and we did not comment or question. This was difficult writing, perhaps the hardest since that first day in September when they had written about personal topics for the first time. I looked around the circle in amazement. There they were, writing fiction like real authors, weaving tales to beguile a sympathetic audience. After everyone had read, there was silence—of respect, pride, and acknowledgment of work still to be done.

The next day, we met again before writing workshop to take stock of how successful students had been in achieving their goals. George was going to add details to his Chuck E. Cheese story to make it sound even more convincing. Chirag planned to introduce a further surprise in his story, "NASA Surprise." Nikhil wanted to explain more clearly why the warriors in his story were rivals. Sanja was going to begin a second chapter of "Looks Aren't Everything." They were nervous, but they were also excited as they prepared to take a run at finishing the first draft.

During the following days I circulated among the students as they worked, not only to find out how their stories were going, but also to learn how they felt about what they were doing. I stopped by George's chair. He is a big, noisy eight-year-old who gallops around the playground and our classroom like an overgrown puppy. His primary-size table and chair are ridiculously small for him. He talks all the time and gets into a lot of trouble, but when George talks about reading and writing, I have learned to listen.

> I thought I wouldn't like writing fiction but that I'd give it a try. When I finished "The Robbery" and read it in the sharing circle, I found that the group liked the story. In fiction, you can make your own things happen. You don't have to use true stuff. If I want to go to Chuck E. Cheese and my dad won't let me, I can do it. If I couldn't write fiction, I couldn't do it.

Like Sanja, George experienced the power and freedom of creating his own reality.

Then I conferred with Chirag, who is passionate about space and dreams of being an astronaut. He explained:

> Almost every book I've read is fiction, and I saw the author did anything he wanted. Two years ago I met a man while I was visiting Cape Kennedy Space Center in Florida. When I got home I imagined he might send me something. I got the idea in grade one, but I didn't know how to write it. In grade two, we weren't into this kind of writing process. Now I know how it feels to be a writer. I used to think of things, but I wondered how writers could write those stories so well. I finally got to write "The NASA Surprise." I'm going to publish it.

Chirag had kept an idea for a story in his head for more than two years. The fiction workshop enabled him to share it. As I moved off to confer with Nikhil, I regretted that I had waited so long to encourage Chirag to try his hand at writing fiction. My nudging had freed him.

Nikhil, another third grader, is shy and tense. He sits for a long time before he writes anything and seldom shares his stories until they are finished. We often wait several weeks to hear from him. Yesterday he had brought his fiction story to the group meeting, and now he remarked:

> I wasn't sure about reading my story to the group because I thought fiction had to be about the future. But I wrote a story that began, "One thousand years ago there were two warriors." The story is about how they were rivals and kept fighting almost their whole lifetime until one died and the other became king. I thought my story would be so different that I wouldn't even be able to answer any questions about it.

Nikhil's story was finished and so clearly written we didn't need to ask questions. I was fascinated by the realm of castles and warriors that had waited in Nikhil's imagination for a chance to emerge.

At the end of the class, Sanja brought her draft to the sharing time. Our veteran fiction writer and self-confessed lover of fairy tales had tried something different in her story about Ellen, a bright girl who felt left out. She commented:

> I tried hard to make a character the group will think is real. I tried to make her do real things in my story. I want to tell people my idea and how I'm thinking. I'm glad I wrote it because it was different from anything I have written before. I think Ellen seems like a real person.

Sanja had solved Ellen's problem by inventing a way for the character to change her appearance. When she read us her first chapter in the read-around, even she was impressed that she could create a plausible character. Until now, she had equated fiction with incredible fantasy.

Two weeks after we had begun, all the stories were completed. Students reported a mixture of feelings about their finished pieces. George said with relief, "I feel happy because it's one of my best. It was the hardest, but I made it through." Nikhil appreciated those first days when I had forbidden comments or questions. He remarked, "I'm glad nobody was asking questions because it was like pushing and they might have spoiled my story." Chirag expressed surprise and pleasure at the positive response to his finished story: "I didn't feel that the group would be interested in a mystery." Karim, who grew to understand that fiction is a blend of personal experience and fantasy, commented, "I'm excited about putting some real stuff together with some fiction." And Sanja said, "I usually write fairy tales, but I'm glad I wrote this story because I think the reader will fall into it."

The ripple effect of new learning continued. Reading journal entries improved almost overnight. Here is George writing to me about Mercer Mayer's *There's an Alligator Under My Bed*:

> This book reminds me of when I was small because I thought there were monsters under my bed. I think this author is trying to make you think about yourself when you were small because he did that to me. When I was small I thought about putting food on the floor too, to make a path out of my bedroom to another room. I actually thought about doing that.

George, now a writer of fiction, put himself into the mind of another writer of fiction, tried to figure out what the author was attempting, and then made a connection with his own early experiences. As Newkirk (1988) would say, George is reading like an "insider" (159).

The beginning was slow. The children had been unsure and so had I. In looking back, I returned to the question I had posed at the start: although they read quantities of fiction, why didn't my students write it? I realized that just as I needed to take a strong leadership role and to structure an environment conducive to individual exploration when my students first began to write personal narrative, so, later, I needed to provide opportunities for them to see the interrelatedness of their reading and writing in encouraging them to write fiction. I needed to draw their attention to the fiction they were reading as a resource for their writing.

Should I have expected a spontaneous transfer from second and third graders' reading to their writing? I believe now that my deliberate focusing of students' attention on the author's craft as they were reading helped to make them aware of themselves as readers of fiction. Noting and discussing what they found that worked or grabbed their interest in particular pieces of fiction gave them authority and the confidence to try this new genre for themselves. When they established their own goals and worked toward them in their fiction, they surprised me with the degree of control they demonstrated. I watched as they mustered their own life experiences, their previous writing, and their backgrounds as readers to produce a new kind of writing. When I guided them in taking a closer look at the fiction they were reading, when I gave fiction writing the importance I had accorded personal narrative, when the group became a community of fiction writers—then fiction writing happened.

Should I have nudged them into writing fiction? It is true that I pushed rather than nudged, but I also left plenty of room for their own choices and judgments. At the appropriate time, I helped them see and present the world through the lens of fiction (Wilde 1985, 130). I took the role of questioner and listened as my students responded with amazing insight. The results were powerful. The rewards were inestimable.

References

Calkins, Lucy. 1986. *The Art of Teaching Writing*. Portsmouth, N.H.: Heinemann.

Francis, Sally. 1977. *Scat! Scat!* New York: Platt and Munk.

Grimm, Jakob Ludwig Karl. 1980. *Hansel and Gretel*. New York: Dial Press.

Kellogg, Steven. 1971. *Can I Keep Him?* New York: Dial Press.

Leaf, Munro. 1936. *The Story of Ferdinand*. New York: Viking Press.

Mayer, Mercer. 1987. *There's An Alligator Under My Bed*. New York: Dial Press for Young Readers.

Morgan, Allen. 1985. *Sadie and the Snowman*. Toronto: Kids Can Press.

Munsch, Robert. 1981. *Jonathan Cleaned Up—Then He Heard a Sound*. Toronto: Annick Press.

———. 1984. *Millicent and the Wind*. Willowdale: Annick Press.

Newkirk, Thomas. 1988. "Young Writers as Critical Readers." In *Understanding Writing: Ways of Observing, Learning, and Teaching*, 2nd ed., ed. Thomas Newkirk and Nancie Atwell. Portsmouth, N.H.: Heinemann.

Parish, Peggy. 1983. *Amelia Bedelia*. New York: Harper & Row.

Peet, Bill. 1961. *Huge Harold*. Boston: Houghton Mifflin.

Rey, Hans Augusto. 1984. *Curious George*. Boston: Houghton Mifflin.

Sadler, Marilyn. 1984. *Alistair in Outer Space*. New York: Prentice Hall.

Sendak, Maurice. 1963. *Where the Wild Things Are*. New York: Harper & Row.

Sharmat, Marjorie Weinman. 1972. *Nate the Great*. New York: Coward, McCann and Geoghegan.

Stevenson, James. 1982. *We Can't Sleep*. New York: Greenwillow Books.

Stren, Patti. 1979. *Sloan and Philamina or How to Make Friends with Your Lunch*. New York: Dutton.

Wilde, Jack. 1985. "Play, Power and Plausibility: The Growth of Fiction Writers." In *Breaking Ground: Teachers Relate Reading and Writing in the Elementary School*, ed. Jane Hansen, Thomas Newkirk, and Donald Graves. Portsmouth, N.H.: Heinemann.

Wildsmith, Brian. 1969. *The Miller, the Son and the Donkey.* London: Oxford University Press.

Williams, Margery. 1983. *The Velveteen Rabbit.* New York: Holt.

HISTORICAL FICTION: THE TIE THAT BINDS READING, WRITING, AND SOCIAL STUDIES

PATRICIA E. GREELEY
Increase Miller Elementary School
Golden Bridge, New York

*W*ho would have thought that fifth graders would think about their writing while lying in bed at night, while riding in the car, while the orthodontist worked on their braces, or during dinner when, in Jennifer's words, "everyone was quiet except for the chewing of food"? I was surprised and delighted to discover that my students' writing had begun to follow them home. Activities that wove reading, writing, and social studies together had captured their interest. They seized the opportunity to manipulate time, place, character, and action within the confines of history by writing historical fiction, which allowed them to go back in time and face life as it was during the 1800s.

Over a hundred years ago in the introduction to *Pioneers of France in the New World*, Francis Parkman wrote:

> Faithfulness to the truth of history involves far more than a research, however patient and scrupulous, into special facts. Such facts may be detailed with the most minute exactness, and yet the narrative, taken as a whole, may be unmeaning or untrue. The narrator must seek to imbue himself with the life and spirit of the time. He must study events in their bearings near and remote: in the character, habits, and manners of those who took part in them. He must himself be, as it were, a sharer or a spectator of the action he describes.

Dates and facts, isolated from people and personalities, cannot depict history fully. Only when they are viewed in the context of daily life can the importance of events be understood, for history is the story of people, the problems they faced, and the solutions they sought. I wanted my students to be actively involved in their studies and to see historical happenings through participants' eyes.

To help my fifth graders envision what life was like during the westward movement, I read aloud such nonfiction books as Russell Freedman's *Children of the Wild West* and Ellen Levine's . . . *If You Traveled West in a Covered Wagon,* and students wrote diary entries as if they were traveling west with the wagon trains.

Then, following steps described by Cora Five and Martha Rosen (1985), the children read nonfiction books about aspects of the early nineteenth century that interested them and investigated topics of their own choosing, which included Indian religious beliefs and practices, the Pony Express, overland stagecoaches, the first transcontinental railroads, fashion, weapons of the period, show folk, and equipment used by cowboys. As a class they brainstormed ways of presenting their information. Their list started with oral and written reports but then branched out to include murals, maps, time lines, models, newspaper articles, interviews, letters, dioramas, diaries, and skits. Each child tailored the options to fit his or her topic.

Kate's presentation combined oral and written approaches. She created a diorama illustrating different methods of gold mining and explained these techniques in great detail in a speech to the class. To give the children an idea of what life was like in a mining camp, Kate read her fictitious journal account of a young teacher, Jeremiah Booker, who left his unruly students in Plymouth, Massachusetts, to strike it rich in California.

Mike became a reporter. After reading several nonfiction books and checking contradictory facts in other sources, he wrote and illustrated his own three-page newspaper. His articles reported on the battle at Little Big Horn and profiled the two opposing leaders, Sitting Bull and General George Armstrong Custer.

In order to learn more about life long ago, the children also read biographies of historic figures and presented projects based on their findings. These projects ranged from a student-made script and videotape of Sacajawea's trek with Lewis and Clark "in search of the shining sea" to fictitious personal letters chronicling the real-life setbacks and achievements of Elizabeth Blackwell, the first woman doctor in the United States.

While the children were reading and working on their projects, they were accumulating a storehouse of information about climate, geography, clothing, food, travel, daily life, customs, and the language of the period. In keeping with Ernest Hemingway's dictum in *Death in the Afternoon,* "A writer who omits things because he does not know them only makes hollow places in his writing," the children wove their knowledge into their stories. Jenny's use of detail in her historical narrative "The Troubles of Elizabeth" transports the reader back in time to the days of the westward movement.

> The day we left was hot and muggy. Perspiration was dripping down my back and my skirts were clinging to the back of my legs. I was so uncomfortable! The wagon train was in a frenzy, all because of my little strawberry blond haired sister Anna. Earlier that morning she had developed a high fever. People feared that Anna might have smallpox and did not want us to join them on the wagon train. So we had to go alone. Mama, her soft face creased with worry, was a little apprehensive about going in the first place. She did not want Anna to get worse. With illness surrounding us, Papa was insistent that we move on and start a new life for ourselves.
>
> If only we had stayed!

Indeed, if only they had stayed. Elizabeth's mother gives birth to a beautiful baby girl during the journey, but the family's joy is short-lived. While down at the river getting water, Elizabeth hears Indians shouting.

Returning to find her mother dead, she realizes that it is up to her to take her mother's place.

> It's not easy filling Mama's shoes. In fact it's harder than I thought. Even though it's been a strenuous journey we've almost reached Oregon. Just last week baby Sarah came down with a fever. With my luck it had to be when Papa had to go away for two whole days to hunt for food. I had to stay up practically all night, constantly rubbing cold cloths on her to bring down the fever. I was so tired. Sarah was just miserable for about four days. Sometimes she wouldn't even eat.
>
> Anna was very helpful when Papa was away. She would help start dinner or start the fire for wash day. I had never realized how exhausting wash day could be. Stirring bundles of clothes in the kettle over a hot fire in the scorching August sun was tedious and tiresome work. It also gave me a backache!
>
> Anna also helped me knit baby booties and sweaters for the up-coming winter, which I hoped to be spending in Oregon! Anna was very hard to deal with during her lessons. For the one hour a day I taught her, she just kept drifting off to another world. She had great difficulty concentrating. I think she misses Mama. I confess I do, too.

Jenny manipulates the plot, forcing her main character to change. Elizabeth must forgo her childhood and take on the role and the responsibilities of care-giver and nurturer. She matures and, for the good of the other children, delays fulfilling her own dreams.

Well aware of her control over her story, Jenny explained her choices. "I wanted my character to have to take over a very important role in the family, something like one of the parents. I knew I had to have Elizabeth's family somehow separated from the rest of the wagon train to create more of a problem."

Isolating her character to heighten dramatic effect is a technique Jenny learned from reading fiction. Like an artist mixing colors on her palette, Jenny used this and other ideas and techniques she had heard and read, blending them together to create a new whole. The social history Jenny needed to be able to write her story did not come from textbooks. It came from biographies, nonfiction books, and historical fiction, which have made the past very much alive for her.

By listening to the historical fiction that I read aloud, the children discovered how much factual information an author has to have in hand before writing a novel. Beyond the facts, the children discussed the main character's growth and the author's purpose in writing the book. In *The Sign of the Beaver* by Elizabeth George Speare, twelve-year-old Matt learns the lessons of survival when he stays alone at the log cabin he and his father have built. When the Indians who have provided companionship and aid move on to new territory, Matt must decide whether he will go with them or remain behind to wait for his long-overdue family. In their reading journal entries, the children examined Matt's changing attitude toward the Indians. They shared their insights in pairs and explored them further in class discussion.

Another thought-provoking book was *Prairie Songs* by Pam Conrad, a carefully crafted story of a young girl who, as she watches a neighbor's wife deteriorate, comes to realize that a settler's survival depends on great inner strength, not physical beauty. In a letter to me, Ryan wrote, "I like the way that Louisa became more mature, and realized that everybody doesn't have to be pretty on the outside, it matters what they are like on the inside." At this point, I asked my students to choose works of historical fiction to read on their own. They selected such books as Eth Clifford's *The Year of the Three-Legged Deer*, Joan Blos's *A Gathering of Days*, Kathryn Lasky's *Beyond the Divide*, Louise Moeri's *Save Queen of Sheba*, and Scott O'Dell's *Streams to the River, River to the Sea*, as well as old favorites by William O. Steele and Laura Ingalls Wilder.

Besides gaining background material as they read, the chil-

dren were exploring the secrets of fiction. In reading workshop
we undertook a careful study of characterization. As the children
read both historical and realistic fiction, they got to know their
characters by examining their actions, words, tone of voice,
thoughts, and physical appearance in entries in their reading
journals.

As a class, we talked about universal story problems. Then
the children created their own story problems and told me briefly
what was going to happen in the historical fiction stories they
were planning to write. Some had to do further research. To
help them avoid creating one-dimensional stick figures dashing
through pages of action (Newkirk 1985), I asked the children
to write character profiles fleshing out their main characters.

Their work triggered a lot of thought. Kate said, "I wanted
my character to make a hard decision about something. I thought
of choosing between parents in a divorce, but I did some research
and realized divorces were very unlikely in the 1800s. So I made
her choose between two races, which was a more suitable problem
for that time period." Her story, "Sarah Edwards, Daughter of
the Moon," began:

> She awoke slowly, trying to sort out the fuzzy shapes that surrounded
> her. "Masake!" she cried. "Tachchu?" She was aware of a sharp pain
> on her forehead and reached up to find a large bump. "Where am
> I?" she thought. She found herself in the middle of a field. As far
> as she could see there were tall stalks of wheat rippling in the breeze.
> Above her the sun was shining radiantly. Off to the side was a small
> soddy with flowers growing on the roof, and a lone tree stood proud
> and tall. "Masake!" she screamed again.
>
> Presently she was aware of voices. "James, do look," said a sweet,
> gentle voice.
>
> "Why, Rachael," said a deep man's voice, "I do believe it's a little
> Indian papoose!"
>
> The baby gazed up at them, smiling. Her dark eyes shone and
> her fine black hair glistened in the sun.
>
> "What a darling baby!" said Rachael. "So much like Joy," she
> added wistfully, thinking of her own baby who had died in the spring.
>
> "Now, Rachael," James said, "how would we talk to her and take
> her in our tiny house and . . ."
>
> But the look in Rachael's eyes told him she would never part with
> the baby.

Years later as Sarah, the main character, sits by the fire em-
broidering a sampler with "Do unto others as they would do
unto you," Indians attack the homestead. James is killed, and

the family is taken to the Indian camp, where a birthmark on her heel identifies Sarah as the granddaughter of the chief. Discovering that white men killed her Indian mother and father, Sarah must decide if she will remain with her Indian grandfather or return to the white family she has grown to love. At the end of the story, Kate wrote:

> She [Sarah] forgave him [the chief] for all the deaths she had blamed him for, realizing for the first time that maybe white people were also responsible for the distrust and suspicion between the two races. Sarah also thought that maybe the white people were to blame for the fighting and that the Indians were just defending their lands and themselves.
>
> As she and Rachael and the children left the village and walked toward home, she knew that part of her would always be Sarah Edwards, pioneer child; but she would also be Nakomis, daughter of the moon, in her heart.

This inner conflict marks Sarah as a three-dimensional character and Kate as an author who has wrestled with character motivation. She freely admitted, "I really had a hard time deciding who Sarah should live with." Kate weighed both sides of the argument. Sarah Edwards/Nakomis comes to an understanding of the adults in her world that Thomas Newkirk (1985) points to as a benchmark for the adolescent author.

Historical fiction was only one of many genres the children tried during the school year. Their personal experience narratives, letters, diary entries, journals, descriptions, book reviews, news stories, poetry, and realistic fiction formed the foundation for the writing that tied into social studies. While they were free to experiment and to use various types of writing, there were times during the year when the entire class focused on a particular genre (Wilde 1985). This exposure kept the workshop approach fresh and vital. It whetted their appetites and challenged them to try something new. Over a period of time, I found that the children included the "new" genre in their repertoire of choices until it joined the ranks of the familiar.

As the children's writing improved, I asked what they thought had spurred them on to new heights. Some students attributed their success to the influence of the books they were reading, to the impact of the books I read to the class, to the mini-lessons in both reading and writing workshops, and to the array of writing genres they tried. Others agreed with Darcy's answer, "We got excited about writing because we were excited about social studies."

While not all fifth-grade authors wrote in as much depth as Jenny and Kate, reading and writing historical fiction did give them an opportunity to step out of themselves. As Donald Murray (1986) writes, "It is important that we read our way out of our own world, our own times, our own skin and live the lives of other people to find out how they feel and think. The ability to distance ourselves and become someone else is a powerful way to learn." The children had a chance to peek into the corners of history and discover that people with needs and wants similar to their own had created our country's story.

At the end of the year when I asked what they had learned during writing, many children cited the different types of writing they had tried, their new awareness of the various options an author faces, and an improvement in the mechanics of their writing. But there were other responses, too. Carey stated, "That's a really hard question to answer. I learned so much about writing. I didn't learn about nouns and verbs, but I learned how to express my feelings in words, in stories, and in a poem. . . . One of the most important things I learned is that I enjoy writing, all because of the way you teach it, I think."

Carey enjoyed writing because she was actively involved in her learning. Allowing her to make independent choices gave her a stake in her work. It unleashed her curiosity and channeled her energy. She felt free to take risks and experiment. This freedom enabled her to explore her powers of critical thinking and fanned the sparks of creativity. The integration of reading, writing, and social studies followed the natural flow of skills, concepts, and content from one subject area to another and reinforced their importance. This is why their writing followed the children home.

References

Blos, Joan. 1979. *A Gathering of Days*. New York: Charles Scribner's Sons.

Clifford, Eth. 1972. *The Year of the Three-Legged Deer*. Boston: Houghton Mifflin.

Conrad, Pam. 1985. *Prairie Songs*. New York: Harper & Row.

Five, Cora, and Martha Rosen. 1985. "Children Re-create History in Their Own Voices." In *Breaking Ground: Teachers Relate Reading and Writing in the Elementary School*, ed. Jane Hansen, Thomas Newkirk, and Donald Graves. Portsmouth, N.H.: Heinemann.

Freedman, Russell. 1985. *Children of the Wild West*. New York: Clarion Books.

Hemingway, Ernest. 1932, 1960. *Death in the Afternoon.* New York: Charles Scribner's Sons.

Lasky, Kathryn. 1983. *Beyond the Divide.* New York: Macmillan.

Levine, Ellen. 1986. . . . *If You Traveled West in a Covered Wagon.* New York: Scholastic.

Moeri, Louise. 1981. *Save Queen of Sheba.* New York: E. P. Dutton.

Murray, Donald M. 1986. *Read to Write: A Writing Process Reader.* New York: Holt, Rinehart and Winston.

Newkirk, Thomas. 1985. "On the Inside Where It Counts." In *Breaking Ground: Teachers Relate Reading and Writing in the Elementary School,* ed. Jane Hansen, Thomas Newkirk, and Donald Graves. Portsmouth, N.H.: Heinemann.

Parkman, Francis. 1865. *Pioneers of France in the New World.* Boston: Little, Brown.

O'Dell, Scott. 1986. *Streams to the River, River to the Sea.* Boston: Houghton Mifflin.

Speare, Elizabeth George. 1983. *The Sign of the Beaver.* New York: Dell.

Wilde, Jack. 1985. "Play, Power, and Plausibility: The Growth of Fiction Writers." In *Breaking Ground: Teachers Relate Reading and Writing in the Elementary School,* ed. Jane Hansen, Thomas Newkirk, and Donald Graves. Portsmouth, N.H.: Heinemann.

WE BUILT A WALL

CAROL S. AVERY
Nathan C. Schaeffer School
Lancaster, Pennsylvania

*A*n unseasonably cold rain darkened the June skies. Inside my first-grade classroom, the children and I gathered on a rug in the corner of the room for our daily literature time. This time of sharing, when we read and talked about books and authors, had helped us to become a trusting, comfortable community during our year together.

China was a unit in our social studies curriculum, and on this morning I read *The Great Wall of China* by Leonard Everett Fisher. When I finished, we paged through the book again, looking more closely at the illustrations. The Chinese characters along the sides of the pages reminded children of our attempts to write in Chinese. The children also noticed red, square-shaped designs on each page, and we found Fisher's explanation of these signatures, called "chops," which Chinese artists use.

My students had heard of the Great Wall and seen pictures of it, but the book provided their first exposure to the history of the wall and its construction. New words such as *barbarians* fascinated the children, as did the descriptions of the wall's dimensions—"six horses wide at the top, eight at the bottom, and five men high." Like the enormous dinosaurs they also loved, the wall seemed so incomprehensible it verged on fantasy. The children's comments during our discussion reflected the awe they felt. But I wanted them to understand that the Great Wall was connected to *people* with problems, concerns, and emotions. It is part of China's history, and history is the story of people. I had an idea that might expand the children's understanding of the wall and the people who built it.

I stood and called out in a deep voice, "I am the Emperor Ch'in. I want a wall to protect China. You will build a wall!" Startled faces looked at me, and then a few giggles broke out. "You! You! And you! Get the bricks, come with me, and begin." I began gathering "workers" and directed them to carry our wooden blocks to the east corner of the room. At first the children were self-conscious, and the giggling continued. "Silence! This is no laughing matter. You must build a wall for China. The emperor has ordered it."

As I maintained the role of the dictatorial emperor, the children quickly became workers striving to build a wall across China—in this case, the length of our classroom—to protect their country from the barbarian hordes.

"Writers, artists, teachers, you may no longer write. You may no longer draw. No more school permitted. You must build a wall for China." The shocked looks that had at first spread across the children's faces disappeared as everyone became involved. In keeping with what we had learned from Fisher's text, lazy workers or runaways were "buried in the wall"—sent to their seats.

The children became resourceful problem solvers as they worked together on the project. When the wooden blocks ran out, they thought of the large cardboard building blocks in the kindergarten room, designated one child to be a messenger to go across the hall and ask to borrow the blocks, and then established a bucket brigade to bring them to the building site. But even the large blocks were not enough; the wall, which curved around desks across the room, was still short. "The boxes!" cried Jason. So they added the boxes that had held the blocks, then finished the last few feet with wastebaskets, chairs, yardsticks, and piles of books.

They completed the wall just as it was time to go to lunch. Afterward, since it was raining, the children returned to the classroom rather than going out to the playground. On their own initiative during free-play time, they went back to Fisher's book and other books on China to search out pictures and read more about the Great Wall. Their research generated improvements to the structure. Tinkertoys and Lincoln Logs became watch towers, and small blocks added ridges along the sides and created a walkway along the top. When Sarah's grandmother arrived early for her weekly session of listening to children read, the children enlisted her as an "inspector" of their construction. She found a tower or two that needed repair before the emperor returned from lunch in the teacher's room. The workers proudly showed the extra features of the structure to the emperor, and I was most impressed.

My students often wrote after we had engaged in a specific activity related to social studies or science units, in addition to the writing they did during our daily writing workshop. A special box held each child's China file, a large piece of folded construction paper that contained individual notes and reflections about our China studies. When they finished the construction, several children retrieved their folders and began to write about building the Great Wall, even before I had returned to the room.

Later, we all wrote for a few minutes, and then we talked about the experience. Writing before discussion was another classroom procedure familiar to my children. I have found that this kind of writing helps children to discover their own ideas before they speak and is particularly helpful to more reticent children. Writing first also encourages children to express their own thoughts without being influenced by others, including the teacher.

In the discussion, the children's responses indicated their personal involvement in the building project.

DUSTIN: Can we do that again? It was fun.

OLIVER: It really looked neat when we were done.

SARAH: Working together was fun. At first we didn't want to, but then we really got into it.

MEGHAN: Working for our country was good.

MARY: I didn't really like the emperor telling us what to do all the time. I was afraid we might miss lunch if we didn't get done.

The following morning during writing workshop, fourteen of the twenty-four children in the class chose to write about the Great Wall of China. I believe that the writing the children had done the previous day, after the role-play activity, captured the experience for them and inspired them to choose this topic during the writing workshop. Children included information about the wall and also expressed their feelings about the experience of building one of their own.

Nicole summarized the highlights of Fisher's text, which the group had focused on during the role-play:

We read a book. It was about the Great Wall of China. Thousands of people worked to make it. The Emperor said, "It will start at north of China and end at the south. The Emperor cracked his whip. "Hey you! Work faster!" People who rested or ran were caught and buried alive in the Great Wall of China. It grew slowly and many were buried alive and many still worked. They worked day and night. It was 5 men high and 10 soldiers across. No one was allowed to rest. And the book ended that no one could go through. The end.

Johnson, a Chinese-American child, recalled factual information brought to life in the role-play:

The Great Wall of China was built by Ti who lived long ago in China. All the people helped build the Great Wall of China. When some people ran away they get buried alive in the Great Wall of China. The Great Wall of China started at the east to the west. The Great Wall of China is old, about 2200 years ago. The Great Wall was to stop the barbarians. China was the oldest country. They had a lots of wall and put them all together and made the longest wall. The end.

In her writing, Kelly identified with the feelings of the slave laborers:

He said, "Get to work." Now, if I was one of them men, I would scream and get (if I could I would) help for my life. When we built the Great Wall in our classroom I felt like I was in jail and no way to escape. I had to work with them. It was fun but I thought it would take us until we were old.

Sarah's spunky personality came through in her writing as she described the building process:

Building the Great Wall was not hard to do because we really got into it once we got interested in it. It was fun working together. If I was one of the workers I would say, "I'll stand up for myself. Humpf!"

Matthew, because of vision problems that required several surgical operations, had come to first grade lacking the experiences with written language typical of a six-year-old. He identified with the hard work of accomplishing this task and the importance of working together.

It was because people helped. You could not rest. You have to work, not stop, all the time. That's why it was hard.

Justin integrated his fascination with the wall's dimensions with his empathy for the Chinese workers.

"Get to work or else I'll throw you in the wall!" I learned that the Great Wall was 4 horses thick at the top and 6 horses thick at the bottom and 5 men tall and every 60 yards there would be a watch-tower 20 feet high and it's 2200 years old. They made mountains of dirt, covered it with bricks and then they put bamboo on top of the bricks on top of the dirt. It felt like I was trapped inside a wall myself.

Oliver and Justin continued to talk about the Great Wall over the weekend. On Monday morning they arrived in the classroom deep in a discussion about the wall. The told me they had played "Great Wall" over the weekend and were trying to figure out how the barbarians could get through.

The boys were eager to tell me their latest theories on the matter. "Couldn't they take long logs and break through the bricks and dig into the wall and make a hiding place in the middle? Then they could make a weak place in the wall, underneath, and it would cave in," they suggested.

"Or they could run around and get through by going around the wall while it was being built," Oliver speculated. Then he mused, "But the book says they *did* attack. It would be neat to tell the emperor that the barbarians could go through it, but way back in those times maybe people didn't think of it."

Later that morning in writing workshop Oliver wrote:

> The Great Wall is not invincible! You can move a block and dirt will come out and you can dig there easy. But when guards are in the watch towers you can't because the guards will get you.

The boys' investigative thinking about the Great Wall of China continued throughout the few remaining days of school. The yesterday of history had become today for Oliver and Justin and their classmates.

The writing and the reactions of the children revealed the diversity of learning that resulted from a common experience. If I had attempted to predetermine a specific objective for the entire group, I would have fallen victim to what Janet Emig calls "magical thinking," a belief that children learn because teachers teach and only what teachers specifically teach. How and what each child learned about the Great Wall was influenced by the interests, personality, and prior experiences of that child. Most of the children grasped the enormity of the construction project, but they made other discoveries that were also significant: the loss of freedom in slavery, the oppression of a dictator, and the threat of barbarians. By reading and talking about a book, using their imaginations in pretend play, and writing about the experience, the children brought new ideas and information to life.

After our initial reading and discussion of Fisher's text, I purposely involved the children in play, a natural human activity that is both personal and social. Using their minds and bodies, they explored ideas and constructed meaning in a highly individual way but in the context of a social transaction. We did not plan *how* to build this wall or *who* was to take specific roles. The children addressed these issues naturally, as they encountered them. Their thinking and talking were spontaneous responses to a collective dilemma. Sharing ideas and listening to each other enabled the children to see other points of view and also highlighted concepts from the book that hadn't been brought out previously.

The wall project might have remained just an activity had it not been for the writing that followed. Writing helped my students discover and shape meaning from their experience. Writing captured the feelings of the moment and propelled their thinking. In years past, I might have ended the activity by assigning a writing task, such as a classbook, or a bulletin board for which everyone drew a picture of the Great Wall. I have come to realize that closure assignments often short-circuit children's thinking and learning, that the imposition of *my* plans prevents children from taking responsibility and subsequently robs them of a sense of ownership of their learning. I have found it more helpful to wait, listen, respond, and trust the children's own capacity to make meaning from the experience using the best tool for learning that I know: language in all its forms.

Through my own writing and observation of children, I have also learned that to focus on finished products and to assign early deadlines may ease classroom management and evaluation, but it does not serve learning. My first graders' Great Wall writing served to nail down their scattered thoughts and impressions and stimulated further thinking. These children knew that not all writing has to be developed for outside audiences, that they could write to record and explore experience, and that they would have time to think and discover a personal perspective before they would be asked to write for me or another audience.

When I read *The Great Wall of China* to the class and began to role-play the Chinese emperor, I did not know how the children would respond. What I did know was that they would learn. Through their collaborative effort and individual writing, they constructed their own meanings of the Great Wall of China.

References

Emig, Janet. 1983. "Non-Magical Thinking: Presenting Writing Developmentally in Schools." In *The Web of Meaning*. Portsmouth, N.H.: Boynton/Cook.

Fisher, Leonard Everett. 1986. *The Great Wall of China*. New York: Macmillan.

FOSSIL HUNTERS: RELATING READING, WRITING, AND SCIENCE

RENA QUIROZ MOORE
Pelham Elementary School
Pelham, Massachusetts

W ant to hear my poem?" Heather asked. She walked across the classroom, sat down as close to me as she could, and began to read:

Roses are red
Snow is white
Here is a fossil
A trilobite!

RENA: Heather, your poem tells me that you know that a trilobite is a fossil. What else do you know?

HEATHER: Nothing much. They lived long ago, but they are all dead now.

RENA: What does your trilobite look like?

HEATHER: You know, a buglike thing stuck in the rock.

RENA: Where did they live?

HEATHER: In the sea, I think.

RENA: If you wanted more information about trilobites, where do you think you could find it?

HEATHER: In a book?

RENA: Anywhere else?

HEATHER: I could ask my mother. She gave me the fossil.

RENA: Those sound like two good places to start. I'll be interested in what you learn.

Heather's poem displayed her strength: she knew a little about fossils and almost nothing about trilobites, but rhymes were her forte. She knew all the jump-rope jingles and classroom songs, much to the chagrin of some of her classmates, especially on

103

long bus rides. While accepting Heather's rhyme as her poem, I also wanted her to know other authors' thoughts and feelings about fossils.

Over the next few days I read the class *Fossils Tell of Long Ago* (1972) by Aliki and *If You Are a Hunter of Fossils* (1980) by Byrd Baylor. We talked about how fossils tell "the finder about life on earth a million years earlier" (Aliki) and how fossils tell us of "some other day that came and went a hundred million years ago" (Baylor). Baylor's book in particular illustrated the sharp contrast between the desert environment where her fossils were found and the sea where the creatures had lived and died.

My second- and third-grade classroom is always a lively place to be, particularly during science time. Most children enjoy "hands-on" science, and the students in my class were no exception. I had started the school year with a unit on geology and prehistoric life that had stimulated student interest and imagination through activities, discussions, and readings. The children had made a time line of the Earth's history, from the "Big Bang" to the present, which wrapped around the walls of the room. In a corner I set up a display of fossils and casts of dinosaur foot-prints, and encouraged the children to bring in others from home. I filled the classroom library area with books on volcanos, dinosaurs, fossils, and rocks. All these materials and activities allowed Heather to integrate scientific knowledge with language arts skills. Here is the second draft of her story, which she read at a sharing circle:

> I do not no mach abawt a fossil
> But I do know taht this fossil is a bug fossil
> It looks like a bug dide on the mud and
> now it is a fossil   Some people call it a
> pacherfid baterfly

Heather then followed our sharing circle custom of inviting responses from her peers.

HEATHER: Do you have any comments or questions?
ELENA: I like how you wrote about the fossil and called it a bug fossil.
SHARON: Why did you call it a bug fossil?
HEATHER: Because it looks like a bug to me.
MARK: How do you know it died on the mud?
HEATHER: I read it in a book.
SHARON: What book?

HEATHER: A book about prehistoric oceans [*In Prehistoric Seas* by Carroll Lane Fenton and Mildred Adams Fenton].
CHUCK: Who calls them butterflies?
HEATHER: Petrified butterflies. Fossil hunters do.
TOM: Where is this fossil now?
HEATHER: In this box. Want to see? I have to hold it. My mother says it's very old and fragile.

Heather walked slowly around the group, showing off her fossil with obvious pride and care. She allowed each child to observe the trilobite, reminding them frequently not to touch it, and then returned it to the fossil table.

Heather had discovered more information about the trilobite and used it to revise her writing. Although it is no longer a poem, the piece is fully her own, written in her voice. She used a text as a resource but did not fall into the trap of adopting the expert's voice. She molded the expository mode of the textbook into her own narrative form. In so doing, she sidestepped a recurring debate: should science facts and concepts be taught directly by the teacher to unknowing students? Or should science be approached as a process through which students learn the skills of a scientist as they observe, measure, record, and experiment? In writing about science, should one use the explanatory, information-giving mode of exposition? Or might one tap the skills of personal narrative and develop one's own, personal science story (Martin and Miller 1988)?

Later, I found Heather sitting on the rug in a corner of the room. Her classmates' comments and questions had stimulated new ideas, and she was engrossed in revising her piece. She was busily crossing out, changing words, and adding new information. "There, it's done," and she read me her finished piece with obvious pride.

My Bug Fossil

I don't know much about a fossil, but I do know that this fossil is a bug fossil. It looks like a bug died on the mud, and now it is a fossil.

My bug fossil, some people call it a trilobite, but I call it a bug fossil because it looks like a bug to me. Other people call it a petrified butterfly.

Now the trilobite doesn't swim or fly. It sits in a box protected by cotton fluff reminding me of creatures paddling through the Paleozoic sea.

Heather's story piqued other students' interest in fossils. They began to observe fossils very carefully and create stories about the creatures who left their imprints in the mud millions of years ago. The two books by Aliki and Baylor mentioned previously, as well as others by Aliki (1969, 1981), Bates and Simon (1985), and Lauber (1987), provided ideas and models for the students to explore. These books illustrate the tremendous explosion of scientific knowledge over the past century. Learners can no longer just memorize facts to be truly knowledgeable. They need to analyze, synthesize, evaluate, and integrate the information they learn. Writing helps develop all of these skills. As we write we recognize new assumptions and previously unidentified implications that are not apparent in the hazy approximations of our memories (Odell 1980). Writing about science allows students "to consolidate what it is they have learned as well as to share with others their discoveries" (Newman 1985). And while writing helps the science student to learn, it also helps the science teacher to teach and guide the student.

Paco had concluded that his seashell fossils were embedded in obsidian, the only black rock he could find on a chart of rocks and minerals. Since he knew that obsidian was formed from volcanic action, he included this in his description of how his fossil was formed:

> A long time ago a volcano erupted and some lava fell in the ocean. Some clams were walking along the ocean floor when a clam got stuck in the cooling lava. Another clam went to help, but that clam got stuck and so on. Years went by. Everyone was gone, and all that was left is the fossil, the print of the shell, I have now.

Only after reading Paco's story did I understand that he had mistaken the black paint on the background of the fossil for obsidian, the rock formed from molten lava. Once we discussed that the seashells may have existed in the bottom of the sea, where sedimentary rocks are often formed, Paco changed his description accordingly:

> A long time ago a group of clams lived in the bottom of the sea. One by one they died and their shells stuck in the thickening mud, and more mud covered them. Years went by. The mud dried into rock. Everyone was gone. All that was left is the fossil, the print of the shell, I have now.

Writing provides me with a way to evaluate my students' learning. Through his description Paco signaled to me that he was unclear about the formation of rocks and fossils. I now knew the facts I needed to emphasize in my conference with him. At the same time, I wondered if other students in the class were also confused by the "black fossils." After questioning the children, I found that one fourth of the class had accepted the black rock as obsidian, even though none of them had included this information in their stories, descriptions, or science logs.

Paco's story led me to develop a mini-lesson on separating fact and opinion in scientific writing. Volcanoes and volcanic eruptions add more excitement and action to a description, but nature also works in quiet, often subtle ways. In scientific writing, factual information must supersede poetic license. The development of scientific knowledge requires critical reading and writing to balance facts with personal ideas and hypotheses. Helping students to distinguish between known information and personal theory and conjecture is one of the science teacher's primary tasks.

The students and I had created a hands-on, meaning-centered classroom in all curricular areas. Together we became active learners and acknowledged ourselves as readers, mathematicians, artists, and scientists through the work and writing we accomplished. Yet I have looked askance as the term "writing across the curriculum" has become one more subject to add to an already packed classroom schedule. I prefer to think of writing and children's writing experiences as tools they can use in many different situations (Murray 1984). What makes more sense for my classroom is "writing *process* across the curriculum." As I reflect on the way I teach reading, science, social studies, and mathematics, I see how conferring strategies, mini-lessons, and sharing circles have permeated each subject. I have tried to extend "the writing process beyond the writing table" and applied "the principles and opportunities of the process to a variety of thinking situations" (Matthews 1985).

Learning is a process in which students integrate old and new information. But too often textbooks, tests, and teachers have structured children's learning, with little regard for the learner. The tenets of teaching writing as a process require stopping to hear the student's voice, observing the process and not just the results, and teaching the writer and not just the writing. In carrying this perspective into the reading class, the teacher listens to the child as a reader, affirms the skills the child possesses, and helps the child to develop new skills and new understanding. And in science, this same teacher sets up experiments and activities, building on the student's previous knowledge, to demonstrate scientific principles. Both the teacher and the student engage actively in the exploration, generating logical explanations for results that can be tested in future experiments. Using a process approach means that students and teachers become involved in lifelong learning.

I know teachers who feel uncomfortable teaching science because their own training included few, if any, science courses. But many of us had these same concerns when we first became writing process teachers. We had to unlearn how we were taught, or not taught, to write. We could still see our graded compositions hemorrhaging with red ink. Then we gathered our courage and began to learn about writing and about ourselves as writers along with our students. The teacher no longer had all the answers; both teacher and students could experiment with new ideas and techniques in an accepting environment: the writer's workshop.

The science workshop likewise allows teachers and students to learn together as we discover scientific principles for ourselves. Peers and teacher are ready to provide support, ask questions, suggest alternatives, point out inconsistencies, and cheer completed investigations. Students become scientists, readers, and writers, not just learners of science, learners of reading, or learners of writing.

From a very early age, children try to make sense of the world around them. Science helps students to see and understand the meaning that exists in that world. In the same way, writing provides students with a mirror to reflect their own thinking about the world, while reading opens the door to others' discoveries, thoughts, and opinions. Fossils and children have many stories to tell if we teachers are only patient enough—and inquisitive enough—to observe and value them.

References

Aliki. 1969. *My Visit to the Dinosaurs*. New York: Thomas Y. Crowell.
———. 1972. *Fossils Tell of Long Ago*. New York: Thomas Y. Crowell.
———. 1981. *Digging Up Dinosaurs*. New York: Thomas Y. Crowell.
Bates, Robin, and C. L. Simon. 1985. *The Dinosaurs and the Dark Star*. New York: Macmillan.
Baylor, Byrd. 1980. *If You Are a Hunter of Fossils*. New York: Charles Scribner's Sons.
Fenton, C. L., and M. A. Fenton. 1962. *In Prehistoric Seas*. Garden City, N.Y.: Doubleday.

Lauber, Patricia. 1987. *Dinosaurs Walked Here and Other Stories Fossils Tell.* New York: Bradbury Press.

Martin, K., and E. Miller. 1988. "Storytelling and Science." *Language Arts* 65: 255–59.

Matthews, Kathy. 1985. "Beyond the Writing Table." In *Breaking Ground: Teachers Relate Reading and Writing in the Elementary School,* ed. Jane Hansen, Thomas Newkirk, and Donald Graves. Portsmouth, N.H.: Heinemann.

Murray, Donald. 1984. *Write to Learn.* New York: Holt, Rinehart, and Winston.

Newman, Judith. 1985. "Mealworms: Learning About Written Language Through Science Activities." In *Whole Language: Theory in Use,* ed. Judith M. Newman. Portsmouth, N.H.: Heinemann.

Odell, Lee. 1980. "Teaching Writing by Teaching the Process of Discovery: An Interdisciplinary Enterprise." In *Cognitive Processes in Writing,* ed. L. W. Gregg and E. R. Steinberg. Hillsdale, N.J.: Erlbaum.

The Author Interview
CAROL AND DONALD CARRICK

AN INTERVIEW BY MARY ELLEN GIACOBBE

*F*ive autumns ago I conducted a writing workshop for teachers who lived and worked on Martha's Vineyard. Halfway into the first morning, Madi Cutts, one of the organizers, informed me that a local author of children's books was present. At first I was elated: a real author of children's books in the audience. Then I panicked. Why wasn't *she* leading the workshop? What if she disagreed with my advice about how teachers could organize writing workshops in their classrooms? And even worse, what would I do if she interrupted me with; "You're wrong! That's not what real writers do." Although I worried that this was the day I would be exposed for not being a "real" writer myself, I managed to say, "Oh, who is it?"

Madi responded, "Carol Carrick." Who is Carol Carrick? What has she written? What will I say to her about her writing? A list of titles of children's books scrolled through my mind until it stopped at *Two Coyotes* and *The Blue Lobster*. Yes, I was familiar with those two books, which made me worry again. I thought of Carol as an author of nonfiction books. Would she dismiss the personal narrative writing that I was describing in this introductory workshop?

If only I had known more about the works of Carol Carrick and her illustrator-husband, Donald, I would have realized that there was little basis for my concern. Over the last twenty-five years, the Carricks have worked as a team on over thirty-five children's books. Donald has written and illustrated seven of his own, and has illustrated twenty-one books by other authors. Their accomplishments have earned them over sixty-eight awards. Their

110

books spread across genres and focus on a variety of topics. Their real-life understanding of how authors and illustrators practice their craft is the basis for the good advice they give when they talk to teachers and children about writing:

> As far as I can see, they [writers] all come to it from a different path, and they all have different methods. Once that became a known fact, you could no longer program schools in the former way of saying ABC is the way to write, because it's sheer folly. There are no rules for being creative. All the writers I know came in backwards, sideways, upside down, and every which way.
>
> Donald Carrick

> That's the one thing I always tell kids—there's no right way to do it.
>
> Carol Carrick

On that fall day I didn't know the Carricks' opinions about writing. Before I left the island I visited one of my favorite bookstores and browsed through the children's section in hope of learning more about the authors from their work. I began to collect their books, and in doing so I became a Carol and Donald Carrick fan. My admiration recently led me back to the island to interview them. I wanted to know about them as writers not just to satisfy my own personal curiosity, but also to share this information with teachers, because the more we know about how authors and illustrators work, the better we can help our students practice the craft of writing.

In my three-hour interview with the Carricks, they revealed fascinating variations in their approach to their work and in their work habits. I asked them how they got started and Don replied:

> I'd been doing illustrations for Bob Goldstein's books, the series on China. I knew the world of illustrating for adult publications. A very lovely editor asked me, why don't you do children's books? It had never occurred to me. I thought of Dick and Jane; I thought of pink and baby blue garbage that I'd remembered. Well, a couple of other editors said I ought to look into it. So I went home and told Carol that if she wrote a children's book, I'd illustrate it.

Carol added:

> I agreed to try to write a book for Don to illustrate. I had no training, which really shows. We hadn't even looked at children's books since we were children ourselves. We hadn't had our first child yet. We didn't know how to do it, or what they should look like, or how they should sound. In some ways, it makes our books rather individual

because they're very personal. Don was a landscape painter when I met him. I had studied art, too. I was an advertising artist of a sort. We were both visually oriented. We just naturally thought of books as landscapes. We used to stay at a friend's house in Vermont. Right across from the house was this beautiful barn. Don started drawing that barn.

Don continues:

> I used the barn and I drew images, and then Carol wrote to them, which is impossible. You can't do that, it's against the rules. It was even hand-lettered. Nobody said, "You can't hand-letter the type." On top of all that, I was doing a three-color, preseparated book, which I had never done before in my life. It's very complicated. You have to do the art three times, then you have to indicate the color to the printer, and I did all of that blind, relying on my own sensibilities, and sent it in. And that is how *The Old Barn* came about. By some marvelous, strange thing, it got a lovely review in *The School Journal*.
>
> We didn't realize that we fell into a classic. Now, we're sophisticated enough to know that if you wanted to illustrate a series of animals, birds, porcupines, and various other things that would occupy an old barn, an abandoned barn would be a marvelous setting. We didn't even know that, we just stumbled on this format. It probably wasn't new at the time and it's not new anymore. We were so innocent when we did it, we felt it looked unique.
>
> When we finished that book I had the best feelings that you could possibly have. I really adored it. Years later the barn burned down and I mourned that barn. I still mourn the barn. We drive by it when we go to Vermont every year, and I can't stand to see that shell, the dry wall. It enrages me. Those temples, those monuments of Vermont are better than anything in the state. Happily, we went by our gut instinct to go toward that lovely subject.

The Old Barn was published in 1966. Almost because they were unfamiliar with the world of children's publishing, the rules did not get in their way. They felt deeply about their topic, and wrote and drew in response to that feeling. This commitment is one of the two things the Carricks have in common with other writers. Throughout the interview, whether they were talking about realistic fiction, historical fiction, fantasy, or nonfiction writing, they returned to the need to know a topic and enjoy it.

The most frequently recurring characters in the Carricks' books are their sons, Chris and Paul. *The Accident* is about a boy named Chris whose dog is killed by a truck. When I first read the story I assumed that it was based on an experience that happened to their son and his dog. Carol told me otherwise:

A few years after we wrote *Sleep Out* and *Lost in the Storm*, we were sorry we had used someone else's dog in these books. We wished we had used a dog we had. I said, "Let's kill him off." So I remembered what had happened to *me* a few years earlier, while I was taking care of a friend's dog. Christopher and his father were out canoeing, and I was coming down to meet them, and that's when the incident in *The Accident* happened.

When I write stories, I use my sons' voices. I know how children talk. But the feelings are really my own. It's like someone owning a boat, a sailboat, and being knowledgeable about boats, so they write sea stories. It doesn't mean it happened on their boat. The fact that we were parents meant that we know what children look like and the way they stand and how they talk. The stories aren't necessarily true. Like with *Washout*: there was a storm up there and trees fell on the house and the road did wash away. But nothing else that happened in the story is true. Christopher did not go out, he did not push a boat around the lake, he didn't hitchhike to the general store, which is a real store. There is a Mr. Humphrey, but none of those things happened to our Christopher.

As the children got older, Carol began to have terrible doubts because she felt she had run out of things to write about. She recalls:

It was a very shaky time, when I thought I had no more subjects. That is when I started reading about history and various topics, some of which became books and some of which never became books. That's how I wrote *Stay Away from Simon*. I was reading American history. Now, I feel that our kids' growing up was probably the best thing to happen, because I have to dig deeper into my own resources.

Carol spent two years doing research on mentally handicapped children in the early 1800s. *Stay Away From Simon* addresses the issue through the eyes of a handicapped child and the children around him and gives readers a chance to think about what it is like to be "different."

Donald's reaction to his sons' growing up was the opposite of Carol's. He knew his subjects so well he could draw them blindfolded, and he looked forward to new challenges as the subjects of Carol's books changed.

For both of them, research is a major part of writing and illustrating. When they were writing *Patrick's Dinosaurs* and *What Happened to Patrick's Dinosaurs*, Donald recalls going to the Museum of Natural History in New York to look at bones and make drawings of skeletons. Carol located as many dinosaur books as she could find and wrote more than most kids would during a year-long research project. She recorded the name of every dinosaur and all the available facts about each. "To look at the simple story that came out of it," she says, "you would never know just how much research went into it." When she wrote *Two Coyotes*, she based it on eighty-five pages of cramped notes about coyotes, deer, rabbits, and owls. Her goal in her research is to know as much about the creature she is studying as anybody alive. As she finds out more about her topic, the facts begin to suggest a story. But Donald thinks it is difficult to go very far with animal books, because, as he says, all animals do is go around finding food and eating it.

Although Carol understands her own need for extensive research, she recalls her impatience with Donald's research for *The Blue Lobster*:

> I couldn't see why he couldn't go to the lobster hatchery and take some photographs. No, we had to have a live lobster in a tank in the studio for a month. I asked him why he couldn't look at photographs of lobsters. But there's this part in the story when the lobster is eating and the food is floating all around. That wouldn't occur to you if you were working from photographs.

I wondered if through the years the process of creating a book had gotten easier, or if the Carricks had learned any tricks to speed up their work. Both answered with a firm "No." Carol worked on a book called *The Elephant in the Dark* for four years. During that time, Donald disclosed, "We were floating in elephant trivia. It was everywhere."

Carol continued:

> All this trivia on elephants. For four years he heard about elephants. Whenever there were elephants on television he would pay attention, and he began tearing out pictures of elephants and collecting them. He was preparing himself, knowing that eventually . . .

Donald interrupted:

> I knew it was going to be set in the early 1800s. I knew it was going to be early barns. I knew it was rural. I knew it was going to have a circus in it. She asked me how one would carry a rifle on horseback, or the logistics of how you would store an elephant and on what floor in a barn you would put an elephant. She had trouble visualizing the barn and where the elephant would be. Carol became completely taken over by elephants. If you listened to her stomping around the house, you would think she was writing a book about an elephant. And the elephant is only one of the characters in that book. She had to know every elephant word. She went to St. Louis and went into the cages with elephants and trainers. She stroked them. She just couldn't get enough. I finally said, "Carol, there is a limit."

She simply replied, "I'd like to spend the rest of my life writing this book and knowing more about elephants. I would love to spend days with trainers; I would love to ride elephants."

At the same time, Donald cautions that knowing too much can get in the way:

> There is a point of no return, where you know more than anyone wants to know. It begins to clog the pores. She's the same way as me, though. She'll say, "But I really have to know, to know what to throw away." We both work that way. I don't want to be reading the book some day and find a hole in it, a flaw. It spoils the book. You're going along in a perfectly good book and this boo-boo is there. I never want that to happen. It's like a frame. It's like you're trying to show off the picture, but all this other stuff is necessary for a vital presentation of the mood that you're trying to create. You shouldn't see it, you shouldn't be aware of it.

Although both Carricks become immersed in a topic, the ways in which they translate what they know to paper are very different. Carol thinks the differences result from the fact that she is an "evening person" and Donald a "morning person." Don says:

> Our relationship works like this. I get up in the morning full of bright ideas. I have my breakfast and go off to work. If I hang around I ramble on and on, and she looks at me as if to say, "Just don't talk to me." When Carol gets up in the morning, she first has to find out if she is alive. About eleven o'clock we can talk and connect, but before then she just doesn't function. She starts functioning in the afternoon and does her best work after dinner or in the middle of the night. When I come in, after working since eight in the morning, she'll start rambling on and on and I just don't want to hear it then. We're opposites.

When Carol is working, her project fills the house. She talks about what she is doing with her women friends and with other writers. She even pumps Paul and Christopher. Carol says, "I love to bounce off people. But unfortunately, you can use up a lot of energy that way, energy that probably should be put on paper." In contrast, Don is very secretive. When he gets a manuscript, he wants to go into his studio and shut the door so that no one will bother him while he creates pictures around sketches or photographs. What he would really like is to go into the studio in the morning, begin the first page, and not come out until the last page is done and he can present a totally completed project. Don feels the same way about writing as he does about illustrating: he just doesn't have a desire for response. However, as Carol explains, "I could go in there and make some comment and I can see later that he has changed the whole book because I have said I don't like something. Even as much as he doesn't agree with me, I can see later that it has pushed him." Perhaps the value of response to a creative artist depends on where the person is in the process, on who is responding, and on the individual's personality.

Don describes another difference in their work habits:

> I have this horrible habit of coming up with a lot of ideas. What I want to do in my method of working is to get all these ideas down and look at them all later, but when the juice is flowing get the ideas out—dump out the bushel basket and look through them. Carol wants to stop and examine every one of these things as they come up. I tighten right up. I just can't do it. I'm trying to tell her "Let it blow." No, she's trying to be accurate. What we realized is that if we each were to write our own books, they would be very different. We each need to do our own thing.

Although the Carricks' work habits differ, the differences don't seem to matter. Carol describes how she writes.

> When I'm writing a long book, I will work every day. Every day, including Saturday and Sunday. I get up in the morning and don't get started for hours. I try to think of ways not to get up there, unless something is going well. With picture books it's hard to get an idea. I can go for a year. I have had years where I just really didn't have a decent idea. But right now I'm working on three books. It's funny, because although I have traveled more this year than any other year, this has been my most productive year. I've gotten to the end of a novel and three picture books.
>
> Picture books are easier because you know before you start that something is going to happen and that it has to end up somewhere. The hard part is figuring how it should end. For instance, I would like to do a story about kids stealing something—going down to the paper store and stealing some small object, because I think everybody has done that. But I can't solve it. So, what happens in the end? If you can figure out what would happen in the end, then you have the whole picture book worked out. With a novel, usually I write about something that I want to know about, like bullies. Very often I start in the middle because I can't figure out how it starts or how it ends. So I just kind of mess around with it. I'll write a scene or a chapter, and if that seems good then I'll write another one. I'm very disorganized, and I write things over and over and over. Now, with the word processor, every day I go up and read what I wrote the day before and perfect it. In a way, I wish I could just sit down and

write from beginning to end. But I don't. It would be nice to write the story and then fiddle with it. This way, I sometimes fiddle with things that never get to be books.

Don observes that, as in her search for a topic, Carol sometimes "gets taken with the beauty of the phrase, and she'll just love the thing. She'll treasure it like little flowers and it will hold her up for four days because she can't, because she doesn't want to not use it. It's like this little jewel. Carol gets hung up on the art of the thing."

Carol agrees wholeheartedly and adds, "It's like doing a sculpture. Say I like the nose, so I just do the nose, the nostrils, the hairs in the nostrils, and the pores. And then I find out later that I can't even use that nose. But I always try to, because I liked it so much. I will try and force that nose in there. Sometimes the editor will say, 'Well, I like it, all except the nose, it has to go.' If you trust your editor, you'll take it out. It's hard."

When it is time to illustrate one of Carol's books, author and illustrator don't always agree. Don claims that

Carol accuses me of illustrating [her books] without reading them. She believes that I give a book a very cursory reading. But I go through it so many times. I read it. I do small sketches and I pin them all up. I look at them and I read it to try to make it flow. With kids you can get redundant, but you never want to repeat. Then I do it larger, and I go through that again. I put the sketches on a wall, move it, change it, and scale it. I go through it again about four times before I get the dummies, even when I go through the final sketch. You can make a great boner in the middle of the book by doing some stupid thing that a kid will catch. I am forced to read it through again and again. It has to be totally true to me to make an entity, a harmonious oneness. Often, it will be almost done, and when you go back and look at it, one drawing doesn't work. So I take it out and make another one. When I'm drawing, I sit there trying to solve the mood of this person in the book. So I am moving his leg, arching his back, I'm just living this guy over and over. Carol says I draw the way she writes. I'm tinkering.

As for my writing, the easiest book I wrote was *Deer in the Pasture*. I literally saw it. I was coming back from painting, driving along a road, and I saw this deer in the pasture with a herd of cows. It was incredibly unusual to me so I followed the whole thing down. I found out who the herd's farmer was, got to know him, and he said, "Come in the barn." The story was written, it was all there. I dedicated the book to the farmer. He didn't quite know what that was all about— a solitary farmer of the old school. I think he was sort of suspicious, but he's been pretty friendly to me.

The first *Harald* book took me forever to do. I became intimidated by all of Carol's writing. I got reams and reams of yellow legal pads, and I sort of had the idea. I would write and write, and this is a cliché, but I would write and my pen would start making pictures. It wouldn't make words. My hand was making pictures, and I would have to tell it to stop, go back, and try to make the words. I enjoyed doing the second *Harald* a lot more. Having color in it: it got more "painty" in a way, and I liked that an awful lot. I suddenly felt for the first time the power that I could really have if I were to both write and illustrate in my own way. I also developed a nifty respect for Carol because I don't use a word processor, I don't type. I would write all this out on the yellow pads. She asked if she could do anything to help, and I asked her to type and print it out for me. She keyed it in without commenting on it, which showed great restraint on her part. She could see all these glaring errors. That was really, really nice. I didn't want her comments.

Listening to the Carricks talk about how they work, I could understand why they believe that there is "no right way to do it [write]." Although each agrees on the importance of knowing a topic, what each does about getting it down on paper is a very personal matter. Each has set up an environment—she in their upstairs bedroom in the corner, and he in his studio thirty feet from their home—that works. Their individual preferences about when and how much they work, when and how much they talk about their work, and what tools they use show why it is so important that teachers allow the "backwards, sideways, upside down, and every which way" that our students may need when they write.

The Carricks caution teachers that the goal in teaching writing is not to encourage children in the belief that they can or will become published authors as adults. Although they are professionals, they stress that the real reason for their writing goes deeper than that. Donald says:

> I write to think. What it proves to me is that I am a person who deals in great, babbling generalities. The discipline in having to put them down helps me to refine my ideas, it makes me crystallize my ideas, it makes me think.

Recently, when I went into one of my favorite children's bookstores, I noticed a new Carrick book: *Left Behind*. The full-color cover shows a young boy in a subway tunnel watching the last car in the train as it moves out of sight down the track. The dust jacket informed me that this new book is the Carricks' eighth about their son Christopher. When I started to read the text, I realized that I was reading it differently because I had talked with the Carricks. I wondered if the story was something that really happened to Christopher, or if Carol was telling her own story. How much tinkering did she have to do to keep the story focused on Christopher getting lost, without going into what happened at the aquarium? Did Donald leave their island home and go to Boston to observe and sketch the subway? The illustrations also had a different look from those in the earlier Christopher books, perhaps because in the last couple of years Donald finally talked his publishers into a full palette of colors. All the same, I couldn't help but get caught up in Christopher's dilemma and how his teacher must have felt about losing a student on a field trip. When I finished *Left Behind* I knew it was another book that children could identify with and enjoy.

Books Mentioned in the Interview

WRITTEN BY CAROL CARRICK AND ILLUSTRATED BY DONALD CARRICK

The Old Barn. Bobbs-Merrill, 1966.
Sleep Out. Clarion Books, 1973.
Lost in the Storm. Clarion Books, 1974.
The Blue Lobster. Clarion Books, 1975.
The Accident. Clarion Books, 1975.
The Washout. Clarion Books, 1978.
Two Coyotes. Clarion Books, 1982.
Patrick's Dinosaurs. Clarion Books, 1983.
Stay Away from Simon. Clarion Books, 1985.
What Happened to Patrick's Dinosaurs? Clarion Books, 1986.
The Elephant in the Dark. Clarion Books, 1988.
Left Behind. Clarion Books, 1988.

WRITTEN AND ILLUSTRATED BY DONALD CARRICK

The Deer in the Pasture. Greenwillow, 1976.
Harald and the Giant Knight. Clarion Books, 1982.
Harald and the Great Stag. Clarion Books, 1988.

ONE OF US

CAROL J. BRENNAN
Madison Middle School
Trumbull, Connecticut

*F*rom the moment the kids stepped off the bus and saw the welcoming posters and mylar balloons, there was an undercurrent of electricity that made it seem as if they were expecting their favorite rock group. But their high was a carefully orchestrated crescendo built through months of preparation—read-alouds, book sales, book talks, bios over the P.A. system. They were about to meet and talk with real authors.

This was the day that Madison Middle School welcomed Paula Danziger, Patricia Hermes, and Vincent Dacquino. When the three authors walked into the small group sessions that morning, the kids stood and cheered. The video cameras were rolling. In the literary world of our school, they were celebrities.

I thought back to the afternoon I had said to the principal, "How about an Authors' Day to bring professional authors face to face with our student authors?" I soon found myself on a committee that also included our librarian and two reading teachers. When we began to consider which authors we might invite, the reading teachers had difficulty coming up with the names of any writers the kids liked. Finally one admitted, "Our kids don't read. They work on skills."

They don't read. The project highlighted the problem, and we began to discuss what we weren't doing with kids in a course called "reading."

Once we had selected three authors, and they had accepted our invitations, teachers began to explore the world of contemporary young adult literature. We read to our kids—many of us for the first time—and we loved it. One of my friends spoke in amazement about the rapt attention of a group of students who normally demonstrated little interest in learning anything. As long as she kept reading Hermes's *Nobody's Fault?*, they listened. I literally bumped into another teacher as she walked to class reading Hermes's *You Shouldn't Have to Say Goodbye*. Instead of apologizing, she murmured, "I've got to find out how this ends."

Since many teachers were reading the same books, we began to discuss the characters and our favorite parts of various novels in the faculty room. We listened to Danziger's tape and chuckled when, during her short career as a teacher, a youngster Krazy Glued his desk to the floor. Together with our students, we gathered every interesting tidbit we could find about the authors' lives and discovered that many books, particularly first novels, are mainly autobiographical. Children found themselves vying with us in buying books, and owning an autographed copy became a universal goal.

We focused on making the day meaningful for the kids, but we also worried about irritating our colleagues by requesting that they interrupt their programs to prepare the kids for the visit. But the teachers were excited too, and this was an unexpected dividend, which the planning committee celebrated. We hoped for acceptance; they surprised us with genuine enthusiasm.

We were equally concerned about the authors. Avi's article, "School Visits: The Author's Viewpoint," published in *School Library Journal* (1987), was extremely helpful. Authors have many horror stories to tell about disappointing visits to schools—when teachers corrected papers during a presentation or, the most frequent complaint, kids hadn't read an author's books. We planned carefully to extend a warm welcome to our guests. The principal would meet them at the door with a greeting and a flower. Parent hostesses would guide them around the school and get them to places on time. We arranged for refreshments, breaks, a catered luncheon, and a private room where they could relax. They weren't just guests; they were honored guests.

Because we wanted every child to have an opportunity to interact with an author on a personal level and a chance to see the authors together to compare their styles, every student in our school of over five hundred students participated in one small group session with fifty or sixty others, and all attended the joint Authors' Forum at the end of the day.

We set up an area for each author for small group presentations. We moved, they didn't. The authors gave thirty-minute presentations, and the remainder of the hour was open for questions and autographs.

In her small group meetings, Paula Danziger talked about her life in a warm, informal way and read the first chapter of a book in progress. It was quite an experience for us to hear an author read from an original manuscript before it was published. The kids felt as though they had attended a premier preview. As Kevin, a sixth grader, told me, "I love knowing what she's writing about before anyone else does, and I can't wait to read it." From her "green jokes" to signing her name backwards, Danziger was a hit.

Patricia Hermes had a delightful way of turning her presentations into living-room dialogue, drawing in teachers as well as kids. She told the kids that she was a spy—mentally recording what they wear and what they say, and always interested in how they feel. "What tricks do you play on each other? What are the in jokes, the latest fads?" she asked. "What *don't* you discuss with your parents? What problems are you dealing with that you'd like to read about in a novel?" The kids watched research in action, and Pat told them, "Some of you will be in my next book." When it was time for autographs, two girls, best friends, bought one copy of Hermes's *Friends Are Like That* and had it autographed to both of them—a tribute to their shared literary experience as well as their friendship.

Vincent Dacquino teaches full time and has published one book, *Kiss the Candy Days Goodbye*, about a boy with diabetes. As Vinnie talked, I found myself wishing we were also videotaping the faces of the seventh graders. I saw many kids, normally as interested in books as they were in past participles, drinking in every word. He talked about being the new kid in a tough neighborhood and taking a dare to jump roofs. This, of course, found its way into his book, and his message that books are about life—our lives—found its way into their souls. He talked about kids who say they don't like to read. "You don't like to read *what*? You may not like green beans, but that doesn't mean you don't like to eat."

At the end of the day, the entire school gathered in the auditorium for the Authors' Forum. Students had previously submitted questions and the committee had selected a number of them, which student volunteers asked from microphones in the audience. (Although it went smoothly, next year we plan a more spontaneous format. By this point kids were so enthusiastic that they had questions they were ready, and brave enough, to ask about issues that hadn't been on their minds when we solicited questions weeks earlier.)

We felt very lucky to have three authors who were personal and open with the kids. When one youngster asked how they coped with bad reviews, Danziger said, "Sometimes I cry . . . and then I say a little prayer: Father, forgive them for they know not what I do." Hermes said that if the first review is good, she can handle anything, but if the first review is negative, subsequent good reviews do not make up for her initial disappointment.

One eighth grader asked, "Why do you write for kids?" "Children are the most fascinating people in the world," Dacquino replied. "They're honest. They're changing. They're struggling with many difficult decisions every day. They're important." Not surprisingly, the kids applauded, cheered, and whistled.

All three revealed that they are often asked why they write for children, the implication being, "If you're good enough, why not write for adults, the important people?" Hermes feels children are always in the back of something—the bookstore, the book review, the sports section. As teachers we felt a common bond with these writers. All of us had chosen professions that put kids in the front row.

Throughout the day, the kids' questions and comments reflected their familiarity with the lives and books of the authors, as well as with the process of writing. As excited as they were, they were not intimidated. Since they themselves wrote every day and were used to having their ideas taken seriously, they spoke writer to writer, understanding the labor that goes into an evolving piece.

As writers they wanted to know why Paula Danziger uses the present tense. And when Danziger asked for feedback on the first chapter of her new novel, the kids treated her as they would a peer author in class, telling her specifically what they liked and why. They discussed believable ways of resolving a conflict she had introduced.

They told Pat Hermes that their writing often goes in a direction they didn't plan, and she said she understood. Her book *Nobody's Fault?* did the same thing. She thought it was going to be about sibling rivalry, but it turned out to be about coping with the death of a sibling. She thought it was her way of working through the loss of one of her own children. Mary, a sixth grader, had read Pat Hermes's book on teen suicide, *A Time to Listen*, and gave Pat a copy of her own story about coping with thoughts of suicide.

These kids were members of what Frank Smith refers to as "the literacy club." When Smith (1986) questioned professionals about how they became writers, artists, scientists, and athletes, they invariably told him the same story: they were influenced by someone who was already a "member of the club" and who admitted them as novice members.

> You have to read like a writer, like a member of the club. It is the only way to learn to write, as any experienced member of the club of writers knows. Exercises in writing sentences and paragraphs—or in filling in the blank—never made anyone an author or even a secretary.

If parents and teachers have already welcomed young people as novice members, professional authors reinforce this apprenticeship with a "Hi, kid, you're one of us." Students become more competent as writers and readers because they *see themselves* as members of the club. They learn at a young age what Anatole Broyard (1988) learned much later in life:

> [Now] I read the book the way I want to read it—I gawk, stare, dawdle, digress, retrace my steps. If the author says something I don't like or can't believe, I argue with him, I refuse to move on till we've had it out. I ask myself how far I should go with the willing suspension of disbelief. Should I suspend my disbelief at all? A good book has a voice and a good reading has voice too.

When the day came to a close, I was sorry it was a Friday. So much energy was going with the kids into the buses, not to return for three days. As one of my students said, "It was a Friday afternoon and kids weren't squirming or yawning. We were just hoping for more."

Teachers lingered in the office—this on a Friday—reliving the day's events and talking about our own reading and writing. One colleague told and retold the story of the seventh-grade boy who returned to class after his small group session with Dacquino and announced, "I have never been so turned on to reading." I thought again of Frank Smith: "The teachers who get burned out are not the ones who are constantly learning, which can be exhilarating, but those who feel they must stay in control and ahead of the students at all times."

Shortly after Authors' Day, Sara, one of my sixth graders, wrote me a note:

> I had been absent for a couple of days last week and let me tell you, was I glad I came on Friday! Pat Hermes was wonderful. I'd love to

have a chance to talk to her alone sometime. While I listened to her, I found that her ideas for books come from everyday happenings. I got a couple of ideas. One of them is a story called "What to Do If a Friend Dumps You." It's about a personal experience I had. I hope that soon (maybe tomorrow?) we can have another day like that.

In June, the kids had their own Authors' Night. They read their best pieces of writing to invited guests, including Pat Hermes, who came to listen and celebrate *their* writing. It was fitting that Gregg read about coping with the recent death of his grandmother. He ended his story with a variation on a line from Pat's book *You Shouldn't Have to Say Goodbye*: "Grandma's dead," he read. "And it stinks." And so we came full circle.

Several of my students were inspired to start their first novels. Nicole called me in the middle of the following summer to set up a conference. She was not only working diligently on her book but was putting aside five dollars a week for publishing costs.

Thinking back to Authors' Day, I remember one seventh-grade boy, whom I didn't know, grabbing my arm and saying, "We *are* going to do this again next year, aren't we?" A thirteen-year-old boy excited not about a rock concert or a football game but about reading and writing . . .

Hey, kid, you're one of us.

References

Avi, and Betty Miles. 1987. "School Visits: The Author's Viewpoint." *The School Library Journal*, January, 21–26.

Broyard, Anatole. 1988. "The Price of Reading Is Eternal Vigilance." *New York Times Book Review*, April 10, 11–12.

Dacquino, Vincent. 1982. *Kiss the Candy Days Goodbye*. New York: Delacorte.

Danziger, Paula. 1974. *The Cat Ate My Gymsuit*. New York: Delacorte.

———. 1979. *Can You Sue Your Parents for Malpractice?* New York: Delacorte.

———. 1980. *There's a Bat in Bunk Five*. New York: Delacorte.

———. 1982. *The Divorce Express*. New York: Delacorte.

———. 1985. *It's an Aardvark Eat Turtle World*. New York: Delacorte.

———. 1986. *This Place Has No Atmosphere*. New York: Delacorte.

———. 1987. *Remember Me to Harold Square*. New York: Delacorte.

Hermes, Patricia. 1980. *What If They Knew?* San Diego: Harcourt Brace Jovanovich.

———. 1981. *Nobody's Fault?* San Diego: Harcourt Brace Jovanovich.

————. 1982. *You Shouldn't Have to Say Goodbye.* San Diego: Harcourt Brace Jovanovich.

————. 1983. *Who Will Take Care of Me?* San Diego: Harcourt Brace Jovanovich.

————. 1984. *Friends Are Like That.* San Diego: Harcourt Brace Jovanovich.

————. 1985. *A Solitary Secret.* San Diego: Harcourt Brace Jovanovich.

————. 1986. *Kevin Corbett Eats Flies.* San Diego: Harcourt Brace Jovanovich.

————. 1987a. *A Place for Jeremy.* San Diego: Harcourt Brace Jovanovich.

————. 1987b. *A Time to Listen.* San Diego: Harcourt Brace Jovanovich.

————. 1988. *Heads I Win.* San Diego: Harcourt Brace Jovanovich.

Smith, Frank. 1986. *Insult to Intelligence.* New York: Arbor House. (Paperback edition published by Heinemann, Portsmouth, N.H.)

PROCESS AND EMPOWERMENT

KAREN WEINHOLD
North Hampton Elementary School
North Hampton, New Hampshire

*J*eremy waited forever for the last day of eighth grade. He knew the legend of "The Boy Who Jumped Out the Window" by heart, and planned to etch his name alongside Ed's, but with a flourish. Only two innocent bystanders had witnessed Ed's spur-of-the-moment decision to leap, but Jeremy announced his intention for months and calculated his audience by the tens. Some days he thought he'd use the west window, nearer the front driveway; others, the east, more clearly visible from the street. Although the distance offered no great danger, he didn't want a sprain, not even a scratch, to mar his performance. In early spring he began daily evaluation of the shrub growth underneath the sills as he contemplated its cushioning effect. From kindergarteners to pregraduates, janitors to assistant principal, everyone knew that Jeremy's jump was going to be his final defiance.

As he approached the open window on that steamy last day, he turned to me and asked, "So, what are you going to do?"— a question he had tossed at me all year.

"What would you do?" I volleyed back.

"Aaugh!" he muttered. His followers recoiled. "You don't quit! First you 'witched me into reading the only whole book I've ever read. Then you keep making *me* find the answers instead of telling me. That's what they pay you for—how come they keep you when we do all the work? I'm gonna tell 'em you're not doing your job. If I jump, somehow you'll find a way to make me write about it. You'll follow me to the high school and ask, 'What did you see when you stood on the sill? Be a camera,

127

Jeremy, take a picture. *Show* the reader what it felt like.' Or you'll find a poem or a pamphlet about 'Jumpers I Have Known,' or I'll have to do research about famous failed jumps, or draft a conversation between me and someone who's afraid to jump. I'm not jumpin' out that window now, no way, and you can't make me."

Phew. Although I knew Jeremy's promise was serious, I had no idea what I was going to do or say when the moment arrived. Now it was over, and I wasn't even sure what had happened, but it occurred to me that using a process approach, putting it back on the learner, had worked again.

It was his small response group in reading that "'witched" Jeremy into reading Theodore Taylor's *The Cay*, not me. They met to debate whether or not the boy and his mother should have left the island, and Jeremy could not join in. He had not read the opening chapters. The others wanted nothing to do with him and dismissed him by pulling their chairs in tighter. I had observed all of this from the sidelines. Soon Jeremy couldn't stand it any longer, and I spied him sandwiching the novel between the pages of his loose-leaf so he could read it unobserved. Surreptitious reading—what next?

Over the past three years, I have transformed the classroom where Jeremy read *The Cay* into a processing center. Everything we do—reading, writing, researching, illustrating, speaking, miming, revising, editing, dramatizing—uses a process approach. Students learn to identify the task, choose and arrange the order of the steps they need to get where they're going, and explore the strategies available to them. Through daily conversation they assess what is working for them and what isn't and change tactics as they evaluate works in progress. The procedure is theirs, and so is the responsibility for making it work. Together we experiment according to individual interest and talent, and share our successes and failures. We collaborate in order to educate ourselves and each other.

Gangly, six-foot Fred carried around a book in a plain brown wrapper, but I wasn't worried. Furtively we met to confer about his choice; he confessed that he had always wanted to read a Laura Ingalls Wilder story. So he did. Soon we were wrangling about the role of arguments in the context of a family. In his dialogue journal he longed for the quiet, undisturbed discussions of this prairie family. In my return letter I asked him if he thought that people who lived together could avoid controversy. Would they even want to? That was the craziest question he had ever heard. Only those who are isolated never have a difference of opinion, I retorted. Student and teacher locked horns. I'd find missives from Fred in my mailbox before school, on my desk after lunch, and, once, stuck under the windshield wipers on my car. The battle waged for nearly two weeks. In the end we were both exhausted and exhilarated, our relationship based on mutual respect cemented forever.

The war did not take place unnoticed. Emboldened by Fred's success in arguing with the teacher, others began looking for debatable topics in the books they were reading. Heredity vs. environment, an issue Katie raised, nearly split the class in two. The "clean needle plan," legalization of drugs, extended school day and year, surrogate parenting, foster children, all lent themselves easily to differences of opinion, and nonfiction books, pamphlets, brochures, and magazine articles became the weapons of choice.

These were soon followed by the "what-ifs" (what if your cousin got AIDS from a transfusion and townspeople threw eggs at her house?) and they began to see how a great deal of fiction develops; they itched to try writing it themselves. The processes of reading, writing, talking, and thinking became cyclical and enmeshed. Now it is impossible to tell where one leaves off and another begins.

Overriding all of this excitement, however, is what teaching this way means for each person in a classroom. A process approach to learning intrinsically meets the individual needs of students as it greets them where they are, encourages awareness of their own strengths and weaknesses, and exhorts them to grow by focusing on what they can do.

Fred was curious about a "girl's book" and knew he'd be ribbed for reading it, so he found a way around the jibing by disguising it. Through our written exchange he expressed an opinion, defended it, amended it, and formed a new one, conscious always of his own role in this critical analysis. Then, with his newly discovered self-confidence, he negotiated a science project that included the physical effects of anger on the human body—not one of the choices listed by his science teacher.

In social studies, Kristy's assignment was to do a report on a famous American woman of the twentieth century. She chose Amelia Earhart and registered her choice with the teacher. In a day or two, after she had investigated the resources available, she outlined her research plans and proposed the direction she hoped to take. Later she discussed her presentation of the material, both its form and its substance. Just as in drafting a piece of writing, all of these plans were open to revision, and she knew that often the final product does not take shape until near the end. Even if Kristy wasted some time and duplicated some effort, she organized her project by herself and next time will probably remember what worked and what didn't. She decided how to capitalize on her own strengths in her presentation and how to minimize weak areas, and she could ask for help whenever she felt the need, with no shame attached. Her teacher coached, listened, and suggested, but Kristy practiced critical thinking and selection. If she does it often enough and in several contexts, Kristy will soon be able to apply these same techniques beyond the boundaries of our school in the larger world.

My entire class made an appointment with the social studies teacher in order to secure more class time for reading Mildred Taylor's *Roll of Thunder, Hear My Cry*, using their collective wiles to point out the historical value of a depression-era novel involving race relations. The next spring, their social studies teacher asked to be given a reading class for the fall.

Katie continues to search for answers to the heredity dilemma, only now she dosn't expect to find someone else's solution. She is amassing data to support her own viewpoint and then plans to write about it. She has confidence in her ability to form and defend her own opinions.

Daily we grow more comfortable with each other, trusting, risking, sharing. In the middle of a letter responding to her reading of Styron's *Sophie's Choice*, Mandy inserts an aside about a very difficult choice she has to make. She pleads with me to tell her what to do. I suggest ways to go about making her decision: listing pros and cons, circling priorities, daydreaming about best/worst scenarios. Now she owns the process again and will develop confidence in her own ability to figure things out.

Reading Neufeld's *Lisa, Bright and Dark*, Derek recounts a time not too long ago when he thought he was going crazy but never dared to share his suspicions with anyone. Now he knows it's okay to be scared, to be confused, not to know answers, to make mistakes. Drafting and revising teaches all of us about the temporary nature of our errors; conferring attunes us to the diversity of valid opinions we hold.

Each of us is important; each has found a way to create success on a regular basis. Self-esteem is nurtured whenever individuals control their lives. A process approach to reading and writing, which routinely empowers students, enabling them to make decisions with assurance, has given me tools to help build their self-worth. And that's why Jeremy turned his back on that window and didn't have to prove himself by jumping. He didn't "just say no." He chose to.

References

Neufeld, John. 1970. *Lisa, Bright and Dark.* New York: Signet.
Styron, William. 1979. *Sophie's Choice.* New York: Random House.
Taylor, Mildred. 1977. *Roll of Thunder, Hear My Cry.* New York: Dial Press.
Taylor, Theodore. 1976. *The Cay.* New York: Avon Press.

CALL FOR MANUSCRIPTS

*W*orkshop is an annual about the teaching of writing and reading. Each volume is centered around a theme and features articles by teacher-researchers of grades K–8, reports of first-hand observations that show a teacher in action and include the voices and writing of students and/or colleagues. Contributors are paid. The editor is currently soliciting submissions to the second and third volumes.

The theme of *Workshop 2* is Beyond the Basal. It will explore a range of ways in which teachers have bypassed publishers' programs to make literature, and students' responses to literature, the heart of their instruction in reading. *Workshop 2* will extend the theories and approaches described in such texts as *Understanding Writing* (Newkirk and Atwell 1988), *When Writers Read* (Hansen 1987), *In the Middle* (Atwell 1987), and *Breaking Ground* (Hansen, Newkirk, and Graves 1985). The editor seeks submissions along similar lines that represent new thinking and practice. The deadline for *Workshop 2: Beyond the Basal* is August 1, 1989.

Workshop 3 will address the Politics of Process. It is intended to help teachers introduce and gain acceptance for process approaches to writing and reading. The editor invites administrators as well as teachers to submit articles to this volume. *Workshop 3* will feature such topics as: curriculum design that supports the development of reading and writing abilities; evaluation procedures that show what children can do; evaluation of teachers who use a process approach; new ways of defining, observing, and recording literacy skills; and approaches to public relations that help administrators, colleagues, and parents understand and support process-based instruction. Again, the focus will be on new work in these and related areas. The deadline for *Workshop 3: The Politics of Process* is August 1, 1990.

Manuscript Specifications for *Workshop*

When preparing a manuscript for submission to *Workshop*, please follow these guidelines:

- Contributors must be teachers of grades K–8 (with the exception of *Workshop 3*), and submissions should be written in an active, first-person voice ("I").
- Contributions should reflect new thinking and/or practice, rather than replicate the published work of other teacher-researchers.
- Submissions must adhere to a length limit of 4,400 words per article (approximately 12½ pages typed double-spaced, including illustrations and references).
- *Everything* in the manuscript must be typed double-spaced, including block quotations and bibliographies.
- References should be cited according to the author-date system as outlined in *The Chicago Manual of Style*.
- Graphics accompanying manuscripts must be camera ready.
- Manuscript pages should be numbered consecutively.
- Send two copies of the manuscript to the editor at the following address:

  Nancie Atwell
  Editor, *Workshop*
  Dogfish Head
  Southport Island, ME 04576

- Include a cover letter indicating for which volume of *Workshop* the manuscript is to be considered, as well as the author's school address, home address, home phone number, and grade level(s).
- Enclose a stamped, self-addressed, manila envelope so the manuscript can be returned, either for revision or for submission elsewhere.
- If the manuscript is accepted for publication, the author will be required to secure written permission from each student whose work is excerpted.

This call for manuscripts may be photocopied for distribution to classroom teachers. The editor invites all interested teachers of grades K–8 to consider sharing discoveries about teaching and learning in the pages of *Workshop*.